NORTH DE'

This guide book contains exact but
wishes to combine visits to such well k
Bideford or Clovelly with an exploration
that lie hidden beyond the better know ..... routes. (For Exmoor, see our
companion guide 'Exmoor Country by Car'.)

The full 'Figure-Eight' Tour shown on the Key Map opposite covers 170 miles, most of which runs through quiet unspoilt countryside (excepting parts of Maps 12 and 13, which are inevitably popularised). This route can be approached with ease from West Somerset, Central Devon, or North Cornwall. You will find that the strip maps show the A roads approaching from the towns, thus giving you an easy link with 'civilization'.

The full 'Figure-Eight' tour is far too long for a day's journey, and we have divided it into North and South Circles. While these both start at Barnstaple, it should be stressed that each route, being circular, may be started at any point suitable. If any particular section of route appeals to you, use the Key Map to plan your arrival at the beginning of the appropriate map.

HOW TO USE YOUR BOOK ON THE ROUTE

Each double page makes up a complete picture of the country ahead of you. On the left you will find a one inch to the mile strip map, with the route marked by a series of dashes. Direction is always from top to bottom, so that the map may be looked at in conjunction with the 'directions to the driver', with which it is cross referenced by a letter itemising each junction point. This enables the driver to have exact guidance every time an opportunity for changing direction occurs, even if it is only 'Keep straight, not left'!

With mileage intervals shown, the driver should even have warning when to expect these 'moments of decision', and if a sign post exists we have used this to help you, with the 'Follow sign marked...' column. However re-signing is always in progress, and this may lead to slight differences in sign marking in some cases... So beware of freshly erected signs.

We have also included a description of the towns and villages through which you will pass, together with some photographs to illustrate the route.

To gain full enjoyment from these journeys be prepared to travel gently and to leave your car as often as possible. North Devon offers a richly varied scene; from quiet lanes and woodlands, punctuated by unspoilt villages and fascinating churches, to the sweeping beaches and towering cliffs of its magnificent coastline. If you are to enjoy these varied treasures to the full, take as long as possible in your exploration... walk along beaches, over headlands to the adjoining bays, wander through woodlands, or amongst remote sandhills. Look inside churches, and stop to chat in village shops and inns, and above all... Don't Hurry!

Compiled by PETER and HELEN TITCHMARSH
Revised by ALLAN and IRENE BLACKNALL
Photography by ALAN and PETER TITCHMARSH

Map 1

kms Ref. Miles   **Directions**   **Signposted**

		Directions	Signposted
A	.0	Depart from The Square, Barnstaple following the signs 'A361 Taunton' round the town's traffic system	Taunton
B	–	Turn left at the traffic lights by the Rose & Crown Inn	Taunton
C	1.7	Fork right off A361 just before garage (WATCH FOR THIS WITH CARE)	Landkey Town
D	.1	Straight, not right	Landkey Town
	.5	Landkey church on left	
E	.1	Turn right at T junction opposite church, and cross bridge over stream	Bableigh Road
F	.3	Over small X rds.	No sign
G	.5	Bear 2nd left at five-way junction, at Bableigh Cross	Cobbaton
H	.3	Straight, not left	No sign
I	.3	Turn left at T junction	Hannaford
	.2	Down steep hill	
	.4	Lovely house on left in Hannaford hamlet	
J	.1	Bear right at T junction, and immediately...	No sign
		Turn right at 2nd T junction	Swimbridge
K	.1	Fork left	Swimbridge
	.7	Enter Swimbridge	
L	.1	Turn right, on to A361	Taunton
		Church on left	
		Jack Russell Inn on right	
M	.1	Turn right at small X rds., off A361, by Methodist Church	No sign
		Up steep hill	
N	.4	Bear left at T junction	Chittlehampton
O	.1	Straight; not left	Chittlehampton
P	.2	Turn left at T junction	Stowford
Q	.5	Bear left at T junction	No sign
R	.4	Straight, not right	Stowford
S	.4	Straight, not right	Stowford
T	.3	Turn left at T junction	Chittlehampton
U	.6	Over small X rds. in valley	Chittlehampton
	.5	Turn left at T junction	South Molton
		Total mileage on this map: 8.9	

TO BIDEFORD
TO ILFRACOMBE
BARNSTAPLE
TO LYNTON
SEE ROUTE DIRECTIONS
TO EXETER
LANDKEY TOWN
HANNAFORD
SWIMBRIDGE
TO BAMPTON
SEE MAP 2

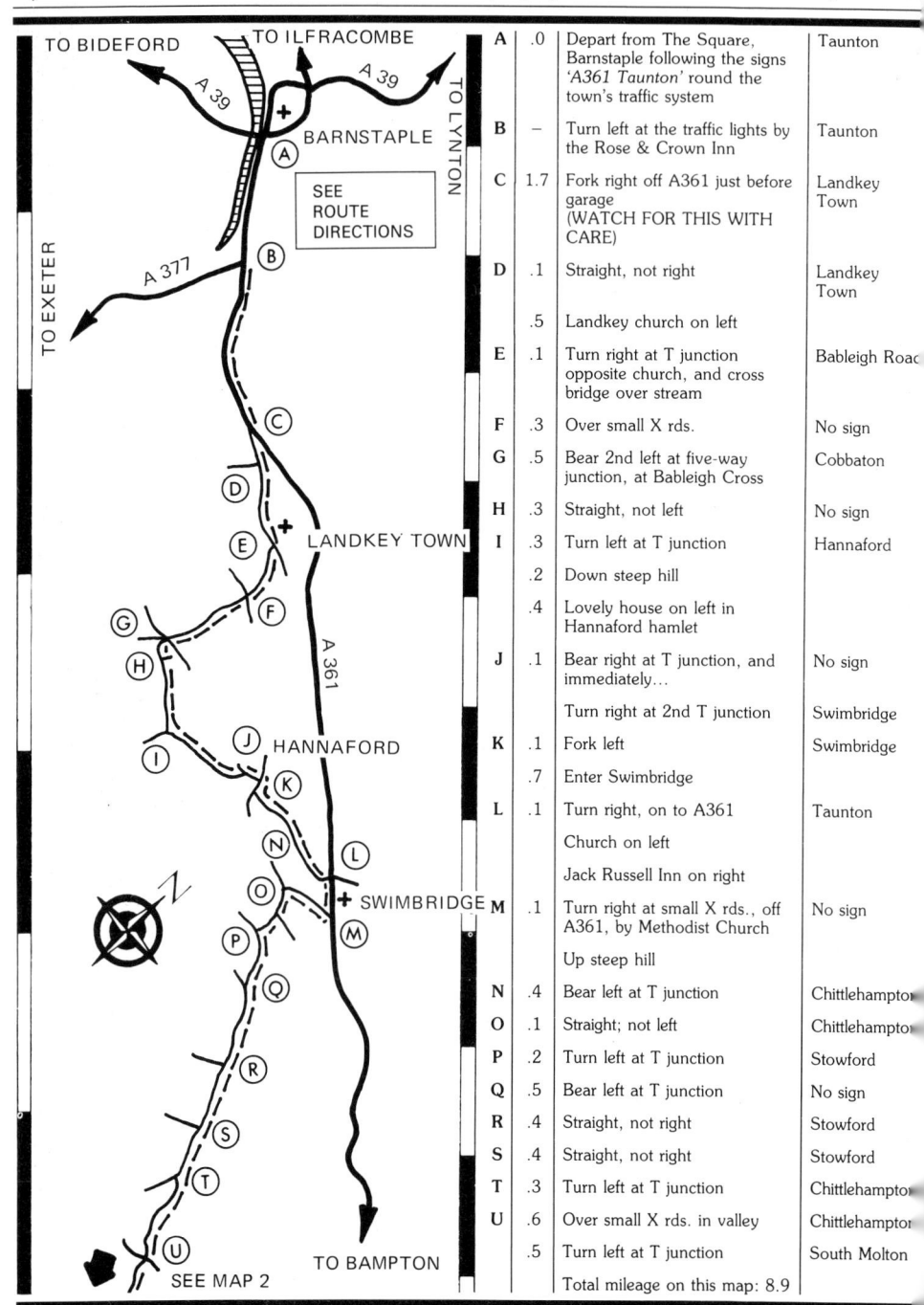

CROWN COPYRIGHT RESERVED

On Route

Barnstaple

Pleasant old town at the head of the lovely Taw estuary, crossed here by a fine 16 arch bridge. Although there is considerable modern development, much of Barnstaple centre is unspoilt, and there is a delightfully unsophisticated air about the whole town.

In the middle ages it was a considerable port, and it was also noted as a ship building and cloth centre. All these activities had declined by the mid-nineteenth century, and until light industries started to spring up a few years ago, Barnstaple existed almost entirely as an agricultural centre.

The church has an attractive lead spire, and looks out across a quiet alley-way to the 14th century St. Anne's Chapel (now a museum), and to the quaint Horwood's Almshouses. Beyond the other side of the church is Butcher's Row, a fascinating mid-19th century street with identical shops, most of which are still used by butchers. Beyond this again is the long covered Pannier Market, which is alive with activity each Friday.

Between the Strand and the site of the old quay stands Queen Anne's Walk, a delightful little stone arcade, dating from 1609, but re-built in 1708. This has a statue of Queen Anne upon its portico and was built as an exchange for the merchants. Do not overlook the Tome Stone, a stone 'table' upon which money was placed by the merchants, thus sealing the bargain in question.

1. Queen Anne's Walk, Barnstaple

2. Landkey Church

Landkey

A small, scattered village whose only redeeming feature is its handsome 15th century church. This has a well proportioned tower and a porch containing a curious roof boss depicting four stags devouring a man's head. The chancel was re-built in 1870, but the nave and aisles have fine roofs, supported on interesting corbel heads, and many charming roof bosses. See also the three medieval stone effigies in the north aisle and the beautifully coloured monument to Sir Arthur Acland and his wife in the south transept.

3. Monument at Landkey

Swimbridge

Sits comfortably in a valley astride the busy A361 (soon to be diverted) with some of its cottages pleasantly arranged on the hillsides. The cheerful 'Jack Russell' Inn lies close to the churchyard wherein lies John Russell, hunting man, breeder of those attractive little terriers, and also vicar of Swimbridge for no less than forty-eight years.

The church has one of Devon's three medieval spires, and it also contains a wealth of interesting interior details, including fine wagon roofs, partly ceiled and painted, one of Devon's finest screens (rather too completely restored for our tastes), a delightfully coloured stone pulpit (c. 1500), and a fascinating font cover and canopy. Do not miss this.

4. Swimbridge Church

5. Detail from Swimbridge Pulpit

Map 2

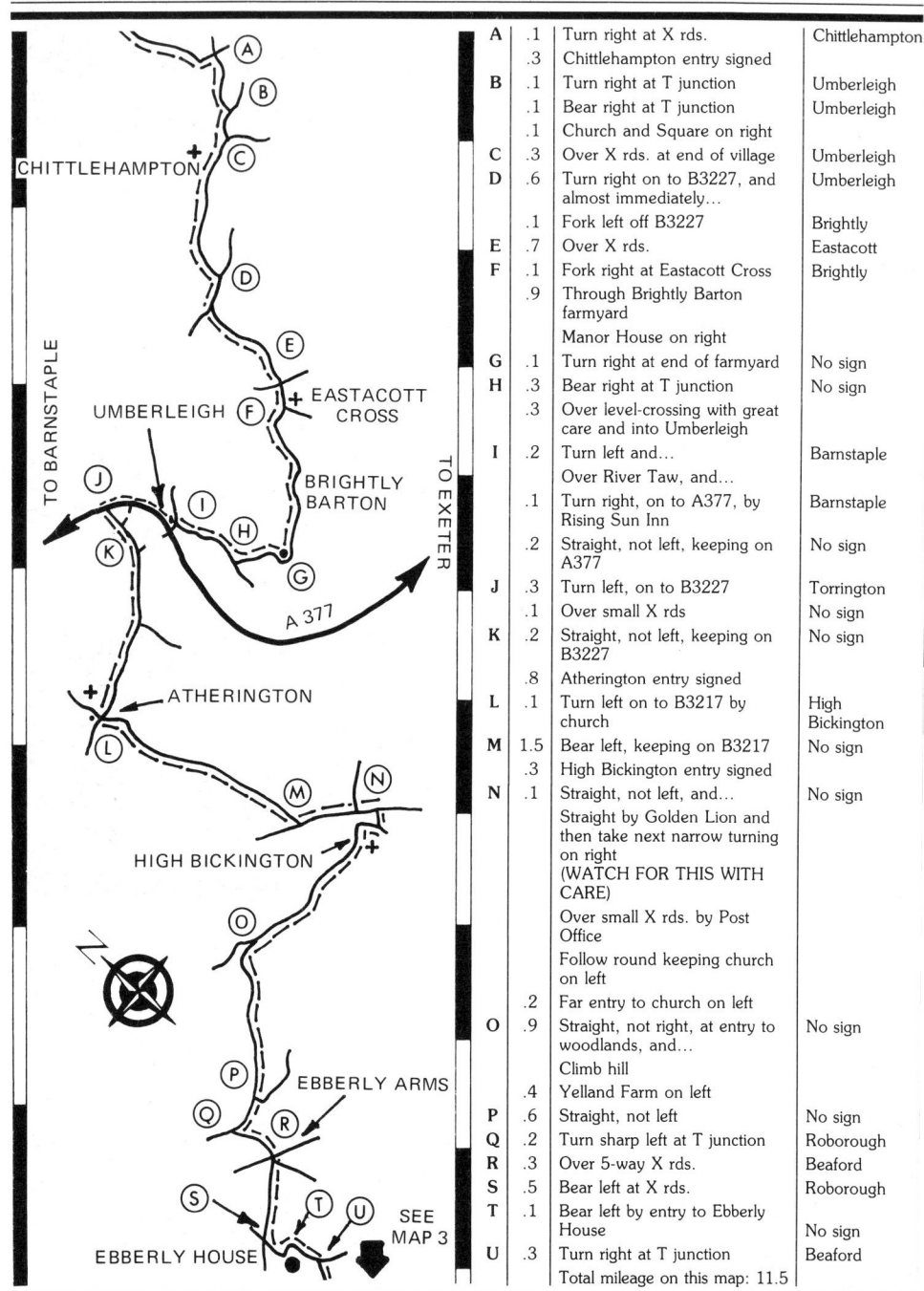

Ref.	kms/Miles	Directions	Sign-posted
A	.1	Turn right at X rds.	Chittlehampton
	.3	Chittlehampton entry signed	
B	.1	Turn right at T junction	Umberleigh
	.1	Bear right at T junction	Umberleigh
	.1	Church and Square on right	
C	.3	Over X rds. at end of village	Umberleigh
D	.6	Turn right on to B3227, and almost immediately...	Umberleigh
	.1	Fork left off B3227	Brightly
E	.7	Over X rds.	Eastacott
F	.1	Fork right at Eastacott Cross	Brightly
	.9	Through Brightly Barton farmyard	
		Manor House on right	
G	.1	Turn right at end of farmyard	No sign
H	.3	Bear right at T junction	No sign
	.3	Over level-crossing with great care and into Umberleigh	
I	.2	Turn left and...	Barnstaple
		Over River Taw, and...	
	.1	Turn right, on to A377, by Rising Sun Inn	Barnstaple
	.2	Straight, not left, keeping on A377	No sign
J	.3	Turn left, on to B3227	Torrington
	.1	Over small X rds	No sign
K	.2	Straight, not left, keeping on B3227	No sign
	.8	Atherington entry signed	
L	.1	Turn left on to B3217 by church	High Bickington
M	1.5	Bear left, keeping on B3217	No sign
	.3	High Bickington entry signed	
N	.1	Straight, not left, and...	No sign
		Straight by Golden Lion and then take next narrow turning on right (WATCH FOR THIS WITH CARE)	
		Over small X rds. by Post Office	
		Follow round keeping church on left	
	.2	Far entry to church on left	
O	.9	Straight, not right, at entry to woodlands, and...	No sign
		Climb hill	
	.4	Yelland Farm on left	
P	.6	Straight, not left	No sign
Q	.2	Turn sharp left at T junction	Roborough
R	.3	Over 5-way X rds.	Beaford
S	.5	Bear left at X rds.	Roborough
T	.1	Bear left by entry to Ebberly House	No sign
U	.3	Turn right at T junction	Beaford
		Total mileage on this map: 11.5	

CROWN COPYRIGHT RESERVED

4

On Route

Chittlehampton

A large village centred upon its fine, wide sloping square, overlooked on three sides by trim cottages, and on the fourth, by a large Perpendicular church. The 115 foot high church tower is claimed to be the finest in Devon, with the strength common to many in the county, but with the delicacy of detail rarely found beyond the western borders of Somerset.

The handsome south porch is approached by a path sheltered by pollarded limes, and there are pleasant views southwards, out over the square. The spacious interior has suffered at the hands of the Victorians, and has indifferent benches, glossy tiles and scraped and pointed walls... all very much in contrast with the unspoilt charm of the porch and the medieval south door. However do not miss the 15th century stone pulpit, the 17th century Giffard monument, and the remains of St. Urith's shrine in the chancel.

It is to St. Urith that we owe the splendours of Chittlehampton. She was born at nearby Stowford in the 8th century and suffered martyrdom at the hands of Chittlehamptonians, who apparently cut her to pieces with scythes. From the time of her death until the Reformation, Chittlehampton was a renowned place of pilgrimage, and this must have largely financed the building of this splendid church.

Eastacott Cross

One of only two surviving medieval wayside crosses in Devon, this is roughly carved out of a single piece of granite, and was probably one of a series guiding pilgrims to St. Urith's shrine at Chittlehampton (See above). The cross stands beneath a beech tree and there are satisfying views northwards over quiet undulating country.

Brightly Barton

A pleasant 16th century farmhouse, once the moated manor house of the Giffards (See Chittlehampton, above).

Umberleigh

The attractive 'Rising Sun' Hotel overlooks Umberleigh's bridge over the beautiful river Taw, flowing northwards to Barnstaple. There used to be a chapel to the manor here, but it was demolished in the 19th century and its monuments were moved to Atherington (See below).

Atherington

We visited Atherington late one February afternoon, and despite penetrating winds from the north-east, were delighted by its hill-top setting. Here is a welcoming village shop and a collection of colour washed cottages around a small sloping square, all dominated by a tall towered church, itself a landmark for many miles around.

Continued on page 7

High Bickington (See Page 7)

1. Cottages at Chittlehampton

2. High Bickington Church

3. Gateway at Ebberly

4. Woodland road beyond Ebberly

Map 3

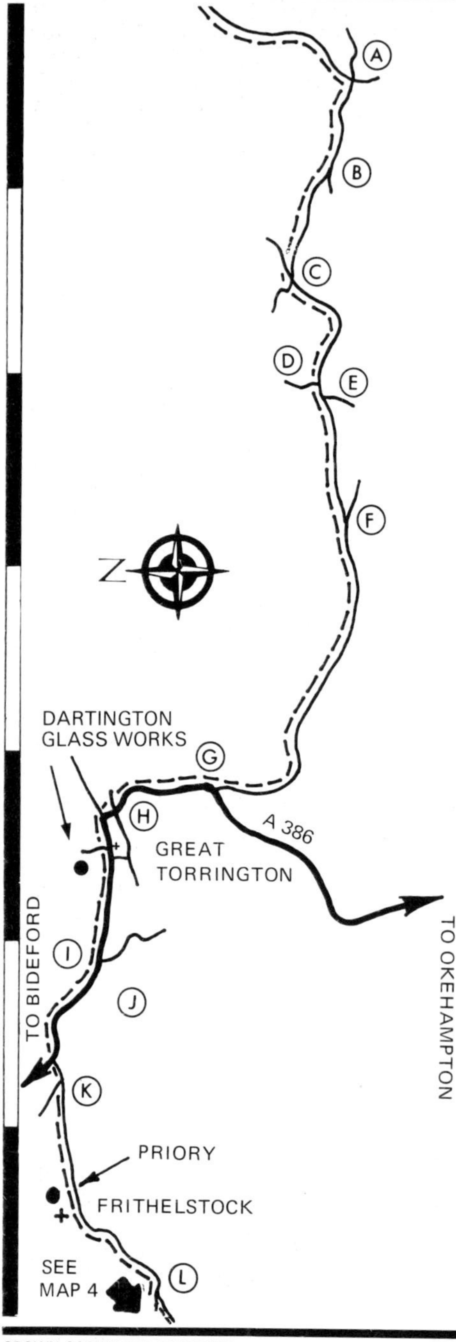

Ref	kms	Miles	Directions	Sign-posted
		.7	Pleasant wooded valley on left	
A		.3	Turn right at X rds.	St. Giles
B		.5	Bear right	No sign
C		.7	Bear left at X rds.	Torrington
		.2	Entering wooded valley	
D		.5	Straight, not right	Torrington
E		.1	Straight, not left	Torrington
			Stream alongside road on left	
F		.7	Bear right on to B3220 (Large parking area on right)	Torrington
		1.7	Torrington spire now visible ahead	
G		.5	Bear right with care on to A386	Great Torrington
			Great Torrington entry signed	
H		.5	Over X rds., and almost immediately...	No sign
			Turn left at mini roundabout keeping on A386 (Keep straight through Torrington on A386)	Bideford
		.2	Church on left (Turn right down School Lane if you wish to visit Dartington Glass Works... .1)	
I		.6	Straight, not left	Bideford
			Pleasant bracken covered country, with Car Park on right	
		.4	Over the River Torridge	
J		.2	Fork left, off A386	Frithelstock
K		.1	Straight, not right	Frithelstock
		.5	Frithelstock entry signed	
		.2	Church and priory remains on right	
			Clifton Arms on left	
L		.8	Straight not right	No sign
			Total mileage on this map: 9.4	

CROWN COPYRIGHT RESERVED

On Route

Atherington
Continued from page 5

Inside the church will be found Devon's only rood loft, complete with narrow winding stair. There is also a series of elaborately crocketed bench ends, a splendid, unspoilt roof, a window full of medieval glass in the north chancel aisle, and several monuments removed from Umberleigh (See Page 5), which include the 13th century effigy of a knight, and a tomb chest with inlaid brass figures.

High Bickington (See Page 4)

The countryside hereabouts appears more Cornish than Devonian in character, and this might also be said of High Bickington, with its cottages and tall thin towered church... all so much more austere than sheltered Swimbridge or prosperous Chittlehampton. Perhaps a February dusk induced this feeling unjustifiably, for once we had entered the Norman south door, we were immediately warmed by the sight of Bickington's amazing series of bench ends... seventy of them, some late Medieval, some early Renaissance, with their subjects ranging from the instruments of the Passion to cheerful looking cherubs blowing trumpets. In a county renowned for its bench ends, it would be hard to find a finer collection.

Ebberly House

An early 19th century Neo-Grecian house, which only reveals itself to us in the attractive shape of the white painted gateway complete with Ionic columns.

Great Torrington

Small town situated on a steep hill overlooking the beautifully wooded valley of the Torridge, and the rolling countryside beyond. The view southwards from the car park close to the bowling green (the site of Torrington Castle) is especially fine, and there are attractive paths lacing across the slopes below, with gorse and bracken covered commons at the western end of the town.

In the town itself there is an unwelcome preponderance of grim Victorian terrace houses in harshly coloured brick and dark granite. The church was unfortunate enough to be blown up in the Civil War, but it suffered more extensive harm in the restoration of 1864, and now has little atmosphere. However we liked the pollarded limes and the cobbled pathways in the churchyard, and the handsome Palmer House close by. This was built in 1752 by John Palmer, who married Mary the sister of Sir Joshua Reynolds.

Do not miss the largely 17th century Black Horse Inn in the Market Square, nor the fascinating Dartington Glass Works, which offers a rare opportunity to see skilled hands fashioning hand blown glass. There is also a shop where the glassblowers' work may be purchased.

Frithelstock (See Page 9)

Continued on page 9

1. Torridge Valley from Torrington

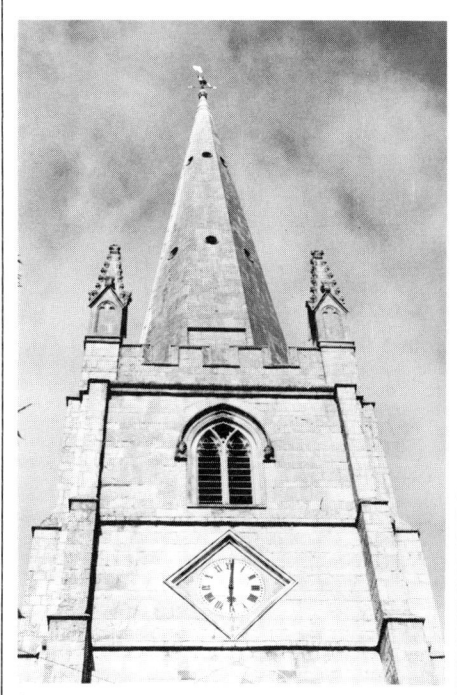

2. Torrington Spire

3. Church and Priory, Frithelstock

Map 4

Ref.	kms	Miles	Directions	Sign-posted
		.1	Turn right WITH GREAT CARE on to A388, and	Bideford
A		.1	Turn left at small X rds., off A388	No sign
		.6	Through Ash hamlet	
B		.6	Turn right at small T junction by single tree	No sign
C		.6	Fork right, over small bridge (Earthworks above right, but not visible from road)	Eckworthy
D		.6	Turn left at X rds.	Holsworthy
E		.4	Straight, not left, at T junction by farm	Holsworthy
F		.1	Bear right	No sign
G		.6	Straight, not right by small chapel	No sign
		.2	Open gorse covered country...	
			This is Thorne Moor	
H		.1	Turn right at X rds.	Woolsery
			Fine views southwards to the outlines of Dartmoor	
I		.2	Turn left	Putford
		1.6	Over small stream	
J		.2	Over X rds.	Putford
K		.3	Turn right at T junction	Putford
L		.4	Turn left at T junction	West Putford
M		1.0	Turn left at T junction, and cross River Torridge	Bradworthy
		.1	Enter West Putford	
N		.2	Turn left, at X rds.	Holsworthy
		.1	Church on right and Manor House on left	
O		.7	Bear right at T junction in Colscott hamlet	Bradworthy
P		.6	Straight, not left, at Thriverton Cross	Bradworthy
Q		.1	Turn left at T junction at Drymoor's Cross	Holsworthy
			Total mileage on this map: 9.5	

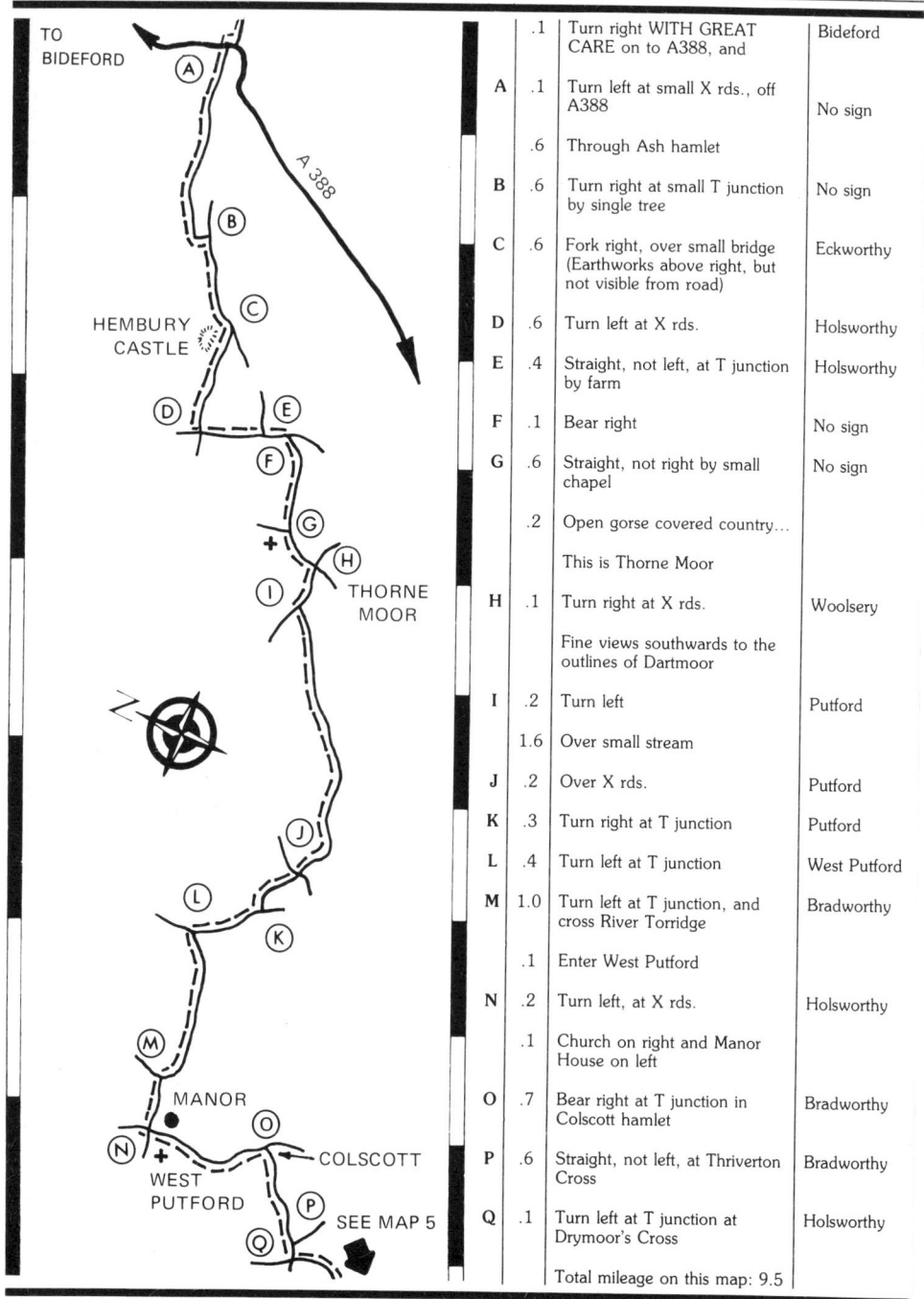

CROWN COPYRIGHT RESERVED

On Route

Continued from page 7

Frithelstock (See Page 6)

Minute village with a brightly painted inn looking out across a small green with daffodils beneath the trees (when we called). On the other side of the road stands the 15th century church, whose handsome, castellated porch is approached by a long path edged with pollarded limes. The interior of the church has a pleasing flavour, with pretty canopied niches in the arcade columns, a Jacobean pulpit, choir stalls with ruggedly carved ends, and more unusually, carved front panels. We also liked the beautiful white plaster Royal Arms, dated 1677.

To the immediate east of the church lie the interesting and beautiful remains of Frithelstock Priory, an Augustinian foundation, colonised from Hartland Abbey (See Page 15). The three lancet windows of the west front are particularly worth noting.

Hembury Castle

An Iron Age Hill Fort to the right of the road beyond Point C. Not visible from the road, and no apparent right of access.

Thorne Moor

A relatively small expanse of open moorland, with gorse and some bracken. There are splendid views south-eastwards to the western flanks of Dartmoor and the rolling countryside of central Devon.

West Putford

A small village with a few pleasantly thatched cottages and an undistinguished bridge over the River Torridge, here little more than a stream. The Elizabethan Churston Manor is situated at the western end of the village, but little of interest can be seen from the road. However the church opposite the manor is full of atmosphere, and is well worth visiting. It lies above and away from the road in a pleasant tree sheltered churchyard, and has a lovely old south door (dated 1620).

The interior is one of the few Devonshire churches to have escaped restoration in the 19th century and is wholly satisfying. It has delightfully uneven, plastered walls, a chancel floor almost entirely covered with Barnstaple tiles, a primitive Norman tub font, and an 18th century pulpit and altar rails. We also liked the monument to Susannah, second wife of John Avery (1689), and the very early woodwork in the north transept.

1. Countryside near Hembury Castle

2. Thorne Moor

3. The Infant Torridge at West Putford

4. West Putford Church

Map 5

Ref	Miles	Directions	Sign-posted
A	.8	Over X rds.	Holsworthy
B	1.0	Straight, not left, by P.O. Box Down steep hill	No sign
C	.4	Turn right at T junction by Post Box, in Sutcombe	No sign
D	.4	Turn left beyond church, which is on right	Bradworthy
E	.5	Straight, not left, by farm	No sign
F	.2	Straight, not right	Bradworthy
G	1.1	Straight, not right	Bradworthy
H	.4	Turn right at T junction	Bradworthy
I	.1	Turn right at T junction at entry to Bradworthy	No sign
	.1	Through Main Square, Church on right	
J	.1	Turn left at end of Square	Morwenstow
K	.3	Fork left	Kilkhampton
L	.7	Straight, not left	No sign
M	.5	Turn sharp left at Stowford Cross	Holsworthy
N	.2	Straight, not left	No sign
O	.9	Turn right at X rds.	Kilkhampton
	1.4	Cross head of the Lower Tamar Lake Reservoir, pass into Cornwall, and immediately...	No sign
		Straight, not right (But turn up right to visit Upper Tamar Lake... Car Park, walks, picnic facilities, shop, fishing)	
P	.5	Turn right at T junction (But turn left and left again, for access to Lower Tamar Lake... under 1 mile)	Kilkhampton
	.8	Pass Forda Farm	
Q	1.1	Straight, not left, joining B3254	Kilkhampton
	.2	Kilkhampton entry signed	
R	.3	Turn right on to A39	Bideford
		Church on left	
S	.2	Turn left, off A39, down West Street, by the War Memorial	No sign
	.6	Motte and Bailey earthwork above us on left but difficult to see from road	
		Total mileage on this map: 13.0	

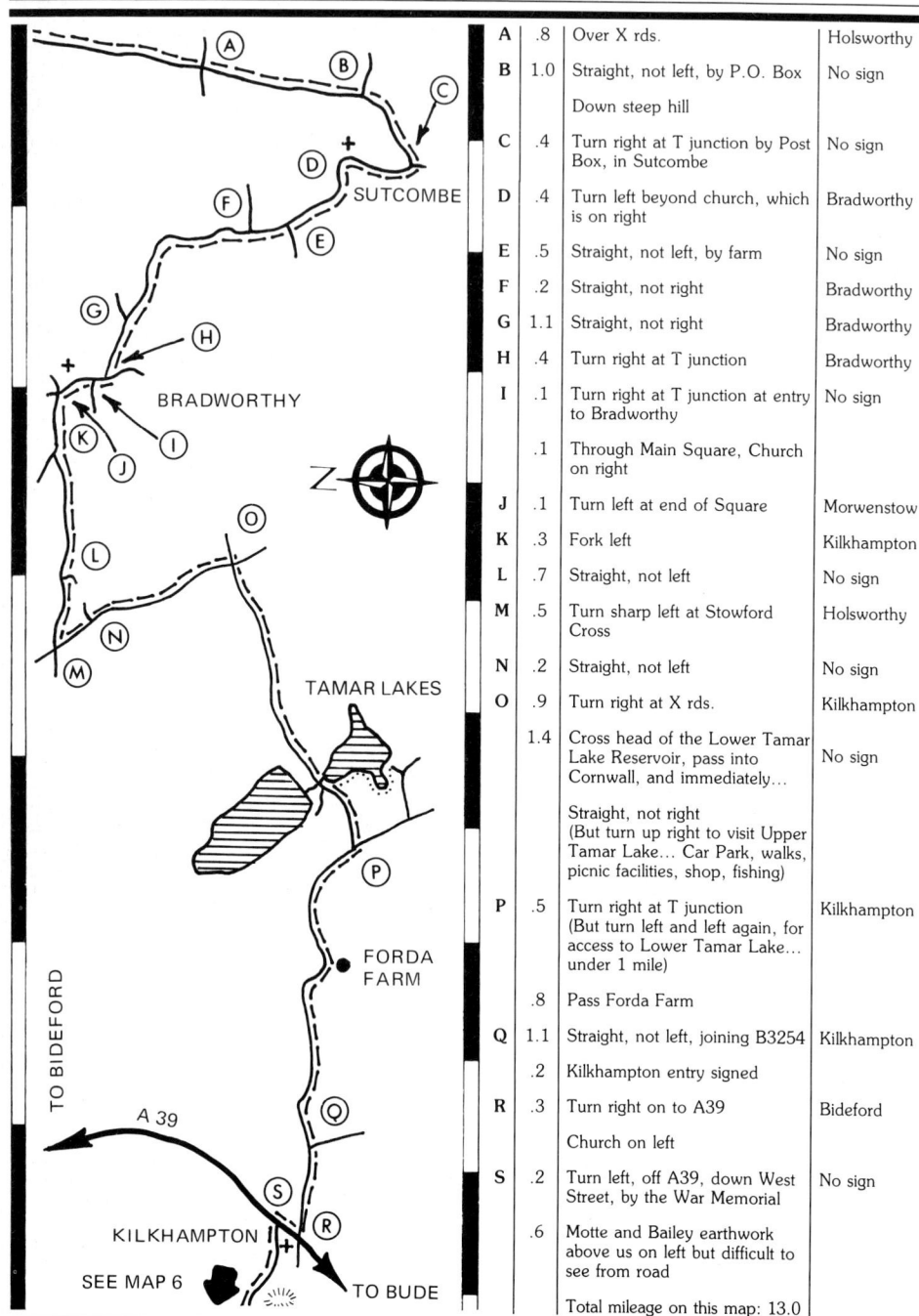

CROWN COPYRIGHT RESERVED

On Route

Sutcombe

Is situated five hundred feet above sea level, looking southwards over unspoilt countryside. We liked the dark grey terrace cottages behind the church and the pleasingly lettered tombstones in the churchyard. Although the tower and south doorway are older, the rest of the church is Perpendicular. It was apparently remote enough to escape the more rabid enthusiasms of the Victorian 'restorers', and retains a most pleasing warmth of feeling. There are many fine bench ends, a well restored screen, and a wide area of Barnstaple tiles, with patterns in high relief. We were also delighted by the gorgeous carved pulpit, with its tall Renaissance panels, and the simple granite arcading. See also the 18th century memorials to Johnathan Prideaux and to his son-in-law, Charles Davie, a man "who really feared God".

1. Winter sunshine at Sutcombe

Bradworthy

A large windswept village grouped around a wide square, whose atmosphere reminds us that we shall be over the border into Cornwall in a few minutes time (See Tamar Lakes, below). The tall church tower looks out over the Bradworthy Hotel and across the square, and leads us to expect an equally handsome interior. However in this we were disappointed, finding it unexceptional apart from the monument to Anne and Susannah Nicholls, and a rather draughty looking late Jacobean pulpit.

2. Church and Inn, at Bradworthy

Tamar Lakes

For most of its length the Tamar marks the border between Devon and Cornwall, and as we cross the bridge below the upper reservoir dam, we move into a new county. Turn up right just beyond this bridge to visit the Upper Lake, where there is a large car park, complete with a shop. There is fly fishing and a dinghy sailing club here.

The Lower Lake is best reached from Point P (See Route Directions) and it offers fine bird watching and coarse fishing. The key to the bird observation hide here is obtainable from the Warden at the Upper Lake, and there is a pleasant nature trail down the western shore of the Lower Lake.

3. Lower Tamar Lake

Kilkhampton (See Photograph, Page 13)

Bright cheerful village astride the A39, with the London Inn well used to catering for the traveller on this busy holiday route. Kilkhampton church is almost entirely 15th century, apart from its splendid Norman south door. It has a handsome tower and a well proportioned exterior generally. The chief treasure of Kilkhampton church is its splendid series of 157 16th century bench ends, one of the most complete in the country. See the Grenville Chapel, whose monuments include that to the Royalist hero, Sir Bevil Grenville, and also the splendidly colourful Royal Arms, a fine example of those given by Charles II to several Cornish parishes to mark their loyalty in the Civil War.

4. Upper Tamar Lake

Map 6

Ref.	kms	Miles	Directions	Sign-posted
A		.4	Bear left at T junction	Stibb
B		1.0	Bear right, and almost immediately...	No sign
		.1	Straight, not left	Coombe Valley
C		.4	Bear right at T junction (But turn left to visit Sandy Mouth... 1.2 miles)	Coombe Valley
		1.0	Coombe Valley Nature Trail starts from car park on right	
		.2	Coombe Mill on right	
D		.1	Bear right beyond bridge (But bear left to visit Duckpool Beach... ½ mile ahead)	No sign
		.1	Straight not right, at Y junction on hill	No sign
		.8	Morwenstow Signal station on left	
E		1.0	Over X rds.	Morwenstow
F		.4	Turn left at X rds.	Morwenstow
G		.4	Bear left at Y junction	Morwenstow Church
H		.4	Arrive Car Park for Morwenstow Church and **TURNABOUT**	
G2		.3	Straight, not right	Bideford
I		.4	Straight, not right	No sign
J		.1	Straight, not left	Shop
K		.5	Straight, not right	Gooseham
L		.4	Over X rds.	Eastcott
M		.4	Straight, not left	Eastcott
N		.2	Straight, not right	Eastcott
O		.5	Straight, not left	No sign
P		.5	Straight, not left, by P.O. Box in Eastcott	No sign
Q		.4	Turn left on to A39	Bideford
		.4	Over offset X rds., keeping on A39	Bideford
		.6	Re-enter Devon	
R		.2	Turn left at X rds., off A39	Welcombe
S		1.2	Over X rds.	Welcombe
T		.2	Fork left	Welcombe Mouth
		.9	The Old Smithy Inn, Darracot, on right	
U		.8	Turn sharp right	Welcombe Mouth
V		.6	Straight, not left (But turn left to visit Welcombe Mouth... ½ mile)	Stoke
W		.6	Straight, not right (But turn right to visit Welcombe church... about ½ mile)	Elmscott
			Total mileage on this map: 15.5	

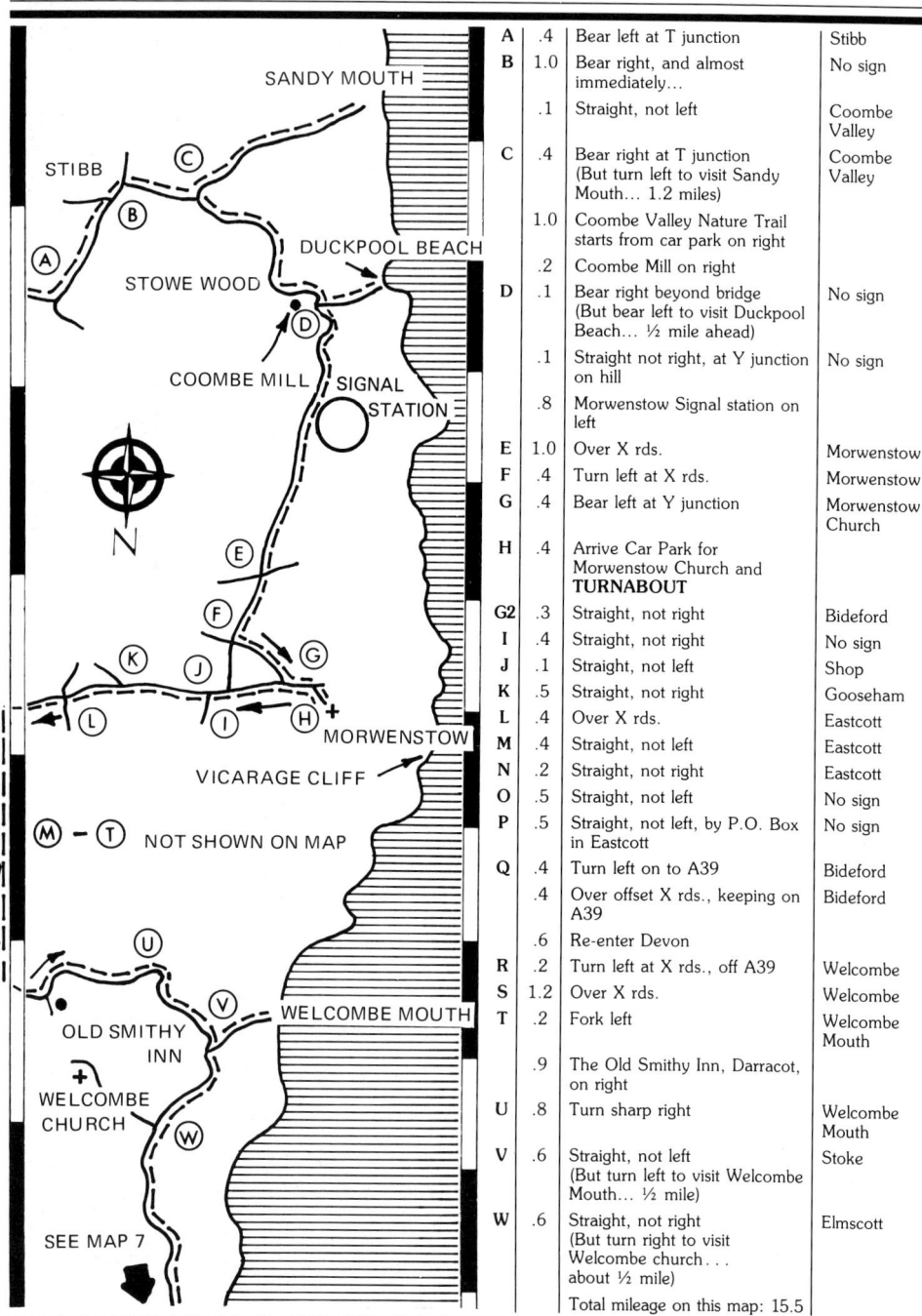

CROWN COPYRIGHT RESERVED

On Route

Sandy Mouth
Our road goes down to within a few hundred yards of the shore, and there is an adequate car park and reasonably sited cafe. At low tide there is a magnificent line of sand, punctuated by jagged rocks, stretching southwards to Bude, and over looked by great gaunt cliffs and the sweeping curves of grassland above. There is a path above the cliffs, northwards to Duckpool Beach (See below).

Coombe
Hamlet with water mill, in the Coombe valley, from whence it is possible to walk up through the Stowe Woods. Parson Hawker (See Morwenstow below) is believed to have written 'And shall Trelawny Die?' while living at Coombe Cottage.

Morwenstow Signal Station
Here are eight great dish aerials in a bleak cliff top setting... a windswept and rather frightening place.

Duckpool Beach and Steeple Point
The north side of this valley is in the care of The National Trust and there is a pleasant small beach with a car park.

Stanbury Mouth
Walk down left from the cross roads at Point E to this pleasant sandy beach (about 1½ miles).

Morwenstow
Church, vicarage and farmhouse stand by themselves at the side of a steep bare valley. The church looks out from its sloping windswept churchyard towards the sea and to Vicarage Cliff, where 'Hawker's Hut' may be found facing out from the hillside. The Reverend R. S. Hawker, theologian, poet and eccentric, was vicar here from 1834 to 1875, and appears to have stamped his personality upon Morwenstow for all time. The hut where he sat for hours, remains, together with his vicarage below the church, with its chimneys built as miniature church towers, and in the churchyard will be found the figure-head of the brig 'Caledonia', put there by Hawker to mark the burial of her shipwrecked crew. When visiting the church, do not miss the primitive Norman font and the fine series of bench ends.

Marsland Mouth
Walk straight ahead at Point U (when the road turns right) for about a mile. The stream below the cliffs marks the border between Cornwall and Devon.

Welcombe Mouth
The road down to the sea is rough, but the scenery provides ample compensation, with the stream pouring over rocky waterfalls to the sea, and high gorse covered hills overlooking the valley.

Welcombe Church
This looks down over the valley from its small churchyard, which was bright with daffodils and primroses when we called. Inside there is one of the oldest screens in Devon (early 14th century), which is crudely carved, but very pleasing. There is also an attractive 15th century pulpit and a Jacobean lectern.

1. Kilkhampton (See page 11)

2. Winter at Sandymouth

3. Morwenstow Church

Map 7

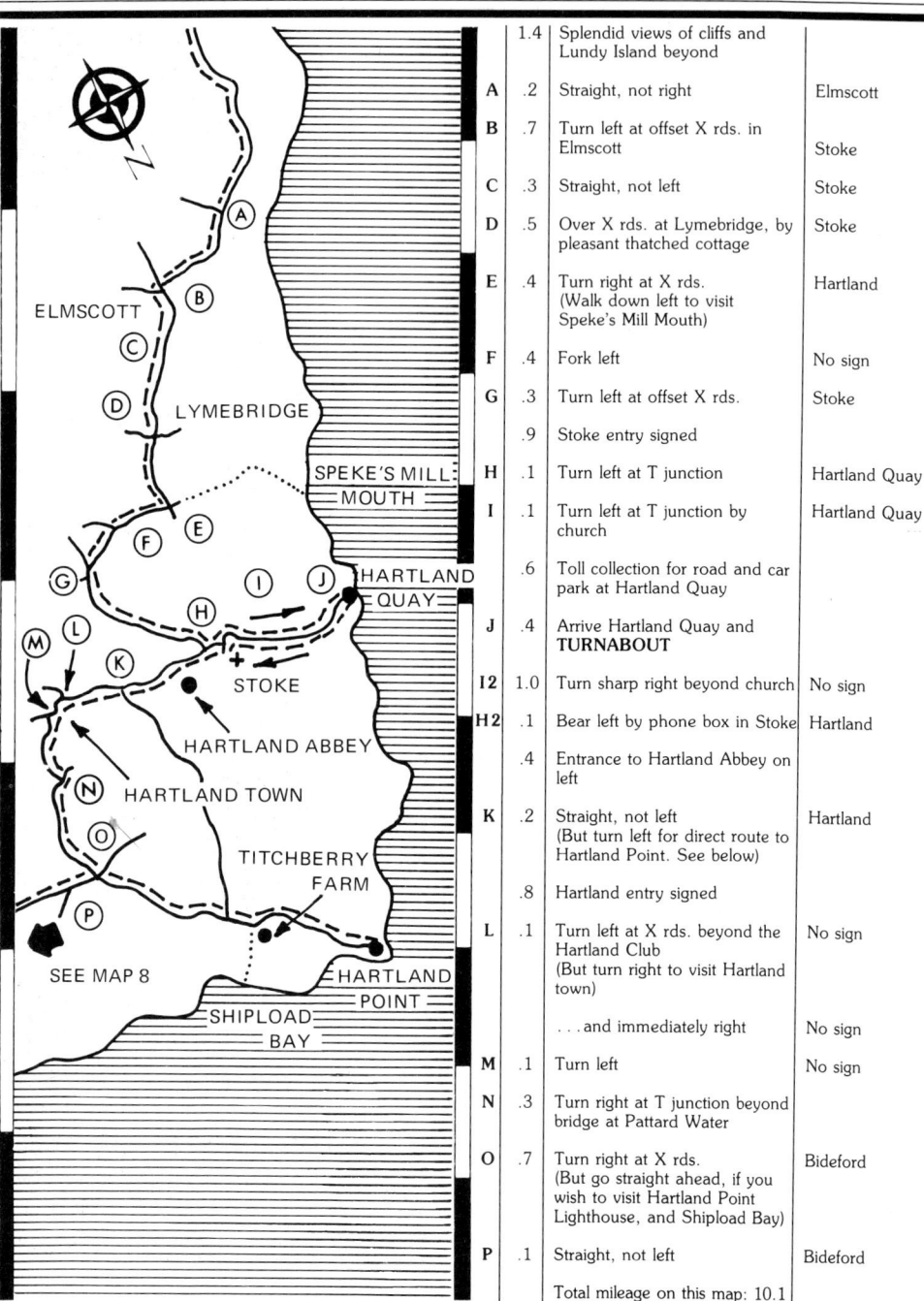

Ref	kms/Miles	Directions	Sign-posted
	1.4	Splendid views of cliffs and Lundy Island beyond	
A	.2	Straight, not right	Elmscott
B	.7	Turn left at offset X rds. in Elmscott	Stoke
C	.3	Straight, not left	Stoke
D	.5	Over X rds. at Lymebridge, by pleasant thatched cottage	Stoke
E	.4	Turn right at X rds. (Walk down left to visit Speke's Mill Mouth)	Hartland
F	.4	Fork left	No sign
G	.3	Turn left at offset X rds.	Stoke
	.9	Stoke entry signed	
H	.1	Turn left at T junction	Hartland Quay
I	.1	Turn left at T junction by church	Hartland Quay
	.6	Toll collection for road and car park at Hartland Quay	
J	.4	Arrive Hartland Quay and **TURNABOUT**	
I2	1.0	Turn sharp right beyond church	No sign
H2	.1	Bear left by phone box in Stoke	Hartland
	.4	Entrance to Hartland Abbey on left	
K	.2	Straight, not left (But turn left for direct route to Hartland Point. See below)	Hartland
	.8	Hartland entry signed	
L	.1	Turn left at X rds. beyond the Hartland Club (But turn right to visit Hartland town)	No sign
		. . . and immediately right	No sign
M	.1	Turn left	No sign
N	.3	Turn right at T junction beyond bridge at Pattard Water	
O	.7	Turn right at X rds. (But go straight ahead, if you wish to visit Hartland Point Lighthouse, and Shipload Bay)	Bideford
P	.1	Straight, not left	Bideford
		Total mileage on this map: 10.1	

CROWN COPYRIGHT RESERVED

On Route

Lymebridge and Speke's Mill Mouth
Lymebridge is a quiet little hamlet in a wooded valley, with a few thatched cottages. Walk down left at Point E for about 1½ miles to visit Speke's Mill Mouth. Here is a small beach with a stream sliding down the sloping cliff into a pool before joining the sea.

Hartland Church, Stoke
The church of St. Nectan, with its 130 foot tower (the highest in Devon) completely dominates the minute thatched hamlet of Stoke. A landmark for miles around, this lofty pinnacled tower has a figure of St. Nectan in a niche in its east face. The church dates from about 1350 and has a spacious interior containing (another superlative) the largest screen in the county, fine wagon roofs, some interesting bench ends, a Norman font, and an elaborate altar tomb.

Hartland Quay
The quay was built in the 15th century to deal with local coastal trade in grain and building materials. It was breached by storms in the late 19th century and as coastal trade had by then declined, it was never repaired. There is a pleasant hotel and some of the most dramatic coastal scenery in Britain.

Hartland Abbey
An 18th and 19th century mansion incorporating the cloisters of an Augustinian Abbey, founded in 1189. It is delightfully situated in a wooded valley half a mile to the north east of Stoke.

Hartland Town
Lost its market status in 1780, and was never nearer than 13 miles to a railway station. Hartland is now only half the size it was a hundred years ago. It is not an obviously pretty place, but its assortment of early 19th century houses and its shops have a certain charm.

Shipload Bay
Park your car at the entrance to East Titchberry Farm (Straight ahead at X rds., Point O, for about 2 miles), and walk down to the small beach at Shipload Bay, one of the very few places on this part of coast where one can reach the shore. There is a dramatic (and demanding) cliff walk eastwards from here to Clovelly, via Chapman Rock, Exmanworthy Cliff, Windbury Point, Mouth Mill and Gallantry Bower (See Page 17).

Hartland Point
(Less than a mile beyond Titchberry Farm.)
This 325 foot high headland forms the N.W. extremity of Devon, with fine views to Lundy and the Welsh coast. The Coastguard Station tops the headland, while the Lighthouse stands on a small 'plateau' 200 feet lower down.

Hartland Forest Information Centre
(See Route Directions Map 8, Point F)
Here is a small Information Centre, from which there is a 1½ mile long forest trail (The Welsford Trail).

1. Near Hartland Quay

2. Hartland Church, Stoke

3. Lighthouse, Hartland Point

4. Shipload Bay

Map 8

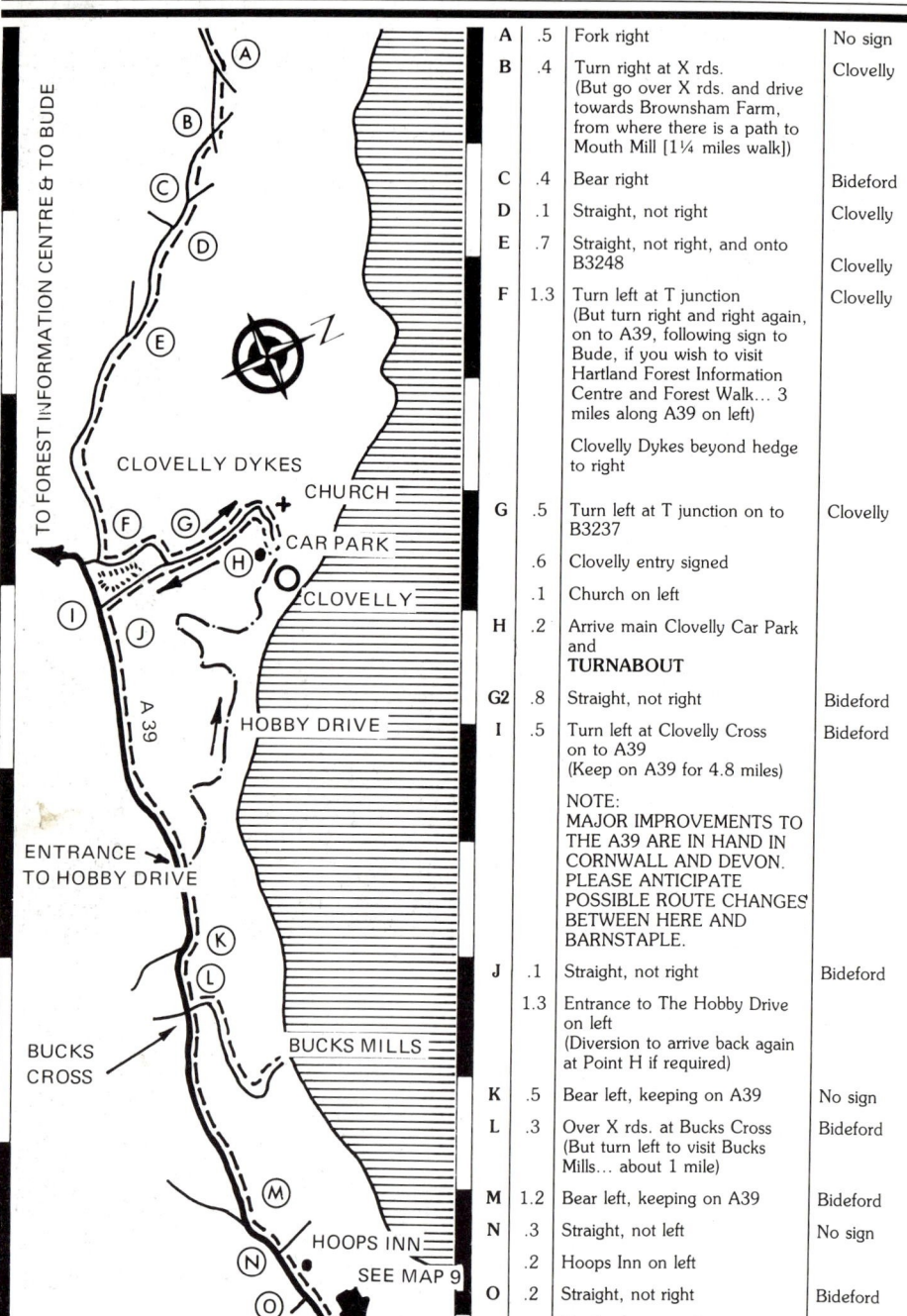

Ref	kms/Miles	Directions	Sign-posted
A	.5	Fork right	No sign
B	.4	Turn right at X rds. (But go over X rds. and drive towards Brownsham Farm, from where there is a path to Mouth Mill [1¼ miles walk])	Clovelly
C	.4	Bear right	Bideford
D	.1	Straight, not right	Clovelly
E	.7	Straight, not right, and onto B3248	Clovelly
F	1.3	Turn left at T junction (But turn right and right again, on to A39, following sign to Bude, if you wish to visit Hartland Forest Information Centre and Forest Walk... 3 miles along A39 on left)	Clovelly
		Clovelly Dykes beyond hedge to right	
G	.5	Turn left at T junction on to B3237	Clovelly
	.6	Clovelly entry signed	
	.1	Church on left	
H	.2	Arrive main Clovelly Car Park and **TURNABOUT**	
G2	.8	Straight, not right	Bideford
I	.5	Turn left at Clovelly Cross on to A39 (Keep on A39 for 4.8 miles)	Bideford
		NOTE: MAJOR IMPROVEMENTS TO THE A39 ARE IN HAND IN CORNWALL AND DEVON. PLEASE ANTICIPATE POSSIBLE ROUTE CHANGES BETWEEN HERE AND BARNSTAPLE.	
J	.1	Straight, not right	Bideford
	1.3	Entrance to The Hobby Drive on left (Diversion to arrive back again at Point H if required)	
K	.5	Bear left, keeping on A39	No sign
L	.3	Over X rds. at Bucks Cross (But turn left to visit Bucks Mills... about 1 mile)	Bideford
M	1.2	Bear left, keeping on A39	Bideford
N	.3	Straight, not left	No sign
	.2	Hoops Inn on left	
O	.2	Straight, not right	Bideford
		Total mileage on this map: 10.2	

CROWN COPYRIGHT RESERVED

On Route

Mouth Mill and Gallantry Bower
A beautifully wooded coombe, dropping down to the rocky coast at Mouth Mill. (See Route Directions opposite for the best approach). It is possible to walk eastwards from here above the 400 foot high Gallantry Bower cliffs to Clovelly (See Below).

Clovelly Dykes
Iron Age 'Hill Slope' fort, the complexity of which is probably explained by the requirement of the occupying tribes for herding their animals in a series of enclosures. The 'Dykes' have not been systematically excavated, but probably date from the 1st century B.C.

Clovelly Church
The path to the south door is overhung by a pleasant avenue of yew trees. The church itself is mainly Perpendicular, although it was heavily restored in the late 19th century, with glossy tiles much in evidence. It is a long narrow building dominated by an exceptional number of wall monuments, mostly to members of the Cary family who held the manor here until the 18th century, and of the Hamlyns, who purchased it from them. Charles Kingsley's father was rector here from 1830–1836, and Clovelly and the Cary family figure in *Westward Ho!*

Clovelly
The North Devon tourist's favourite place of pilgrimage for many generations, Clovelly appears to have withstood the consequent pressures remarkably well. It has a long cobbled street, so steep in places that it has had to be stepped, descending to a small harbour with a stout stone pier. Attractive cottages and shops crowd in upon the narrow little street as it drops towards the harbour and towering above it all there are splendidly wooded cliffs.

At the very bottom of the street there is an old inn, which is situated at the harbour's edge. There are inevitable trips 'round the bay', and the less energetic will be relieved to know that they are not bound to walk back up through the village. (There is a Landrover service up a road to the west of the village which will return you to the car park.)

The Hobby Drive
(See Route Directions for access details.)

Splendid three mile wooded coastal 'drive' built in the 19th century by Sir James Hamlyn, the Lord of the Manor of Clovelly. When we last drove this way the roadway was rather rough in places, but for all this, the toll charge is more than justified by the glorious views out across to Bideford Bay and down through the trees to Clovelly far below. Do not miss this.

Bucks Mills
A good road leads down the wooded valley to a Forestry Commission car park. It is advisable to leave the car here and walk to the collection of cottages which have a flavour of South Cornwall. Just beyond there is a rock strewn, shingly beach, with a little sand.

1. Clovelly Harbour

2. Clovelly

3. On the Hobby Drive

Map 9

Ref	kms/Miles	Directions	Signposted
A	.3	Straight, not left, by Horns Cross entry	Bideford
	.1	Turn right at X rds., off A39 **(Watch for this, with care)**	Parkham
B	.7	Bear left in Goldworthy hamlet	Buckland
	.1	Straight, not left	No sign
C	.5	Bear left at T junction	Bideford
D	.1	Straight, not right	No sign
E	.2	Straight, not right	No sign
F	1.1	Bear right	Bideford
G	.3	Bear left, and...	Bideford
		Bear left again immediately beyond bridge, and...	No sign
	.2	Straight, not right, by Groves Cross Cottage	No sign
H	.4	Turn left at X rds.	Abbotsham
I	.7	Straight, not left	
J	.7	Turn left...	No sign
		and immediately straight at roundabout, crossing the A39	Abbotsham
K	.4	Abbotsham entry sign	
L	.3	Over X rds. by church	Westward Ho!
	.2	Over 2nd X rds.	No sign
M	.4	Over 3rd X rds.	Westward Ho!
N	.2	Straight, not left	Westward Ho!
O	.3	Straight, not right	Westward Ho!
P	.3	Turn left at T junction	Westward Ho!
	.3	Straight, not right	Westward Ho!
	.2	Westward Ho! entry sign	
Q	.2	Over X rds.	Westward Ho!
R	.3	Bear round to right, by Golden Bay House	No sign
	.1	Bear left into one-way system (Keep on B3236, through Westward Ho!)	No sign
S	.3	Bear left at Y junction	Northam
	.7	Turn left off Northam by-pass	Northam Town Centre
T	.3	Turn left by Northam P.O. and immediately...	No sign
		Bear right (Keep straight out on this road)	Appledore
	.3	Fork left by speed de-restriction sign (NOT Diddywell Road)	No sign
	.1	Turn right at T junction... and keep straight not right	No sign
U	.2	Over offset X rds.	Appledore
V	.3	Straight, not right	No sign
	.1	Over small X rds.	No sign
	.5	Entering Appledore	
	.7	Maritime Museum signed up to right	
W	.2	Bear round left beyond 1st shipyard, by British Legion Club	No sign
X	.8	Straight, not right	No sign
	.1	Turn left on to B3236	No sign
	.4	Entering Northam	
Y	.5	Turn left on to A386	Bideford
	.1	Straight, not left, keeping on A386	No sign
		Total mileage on this map: 13.7	

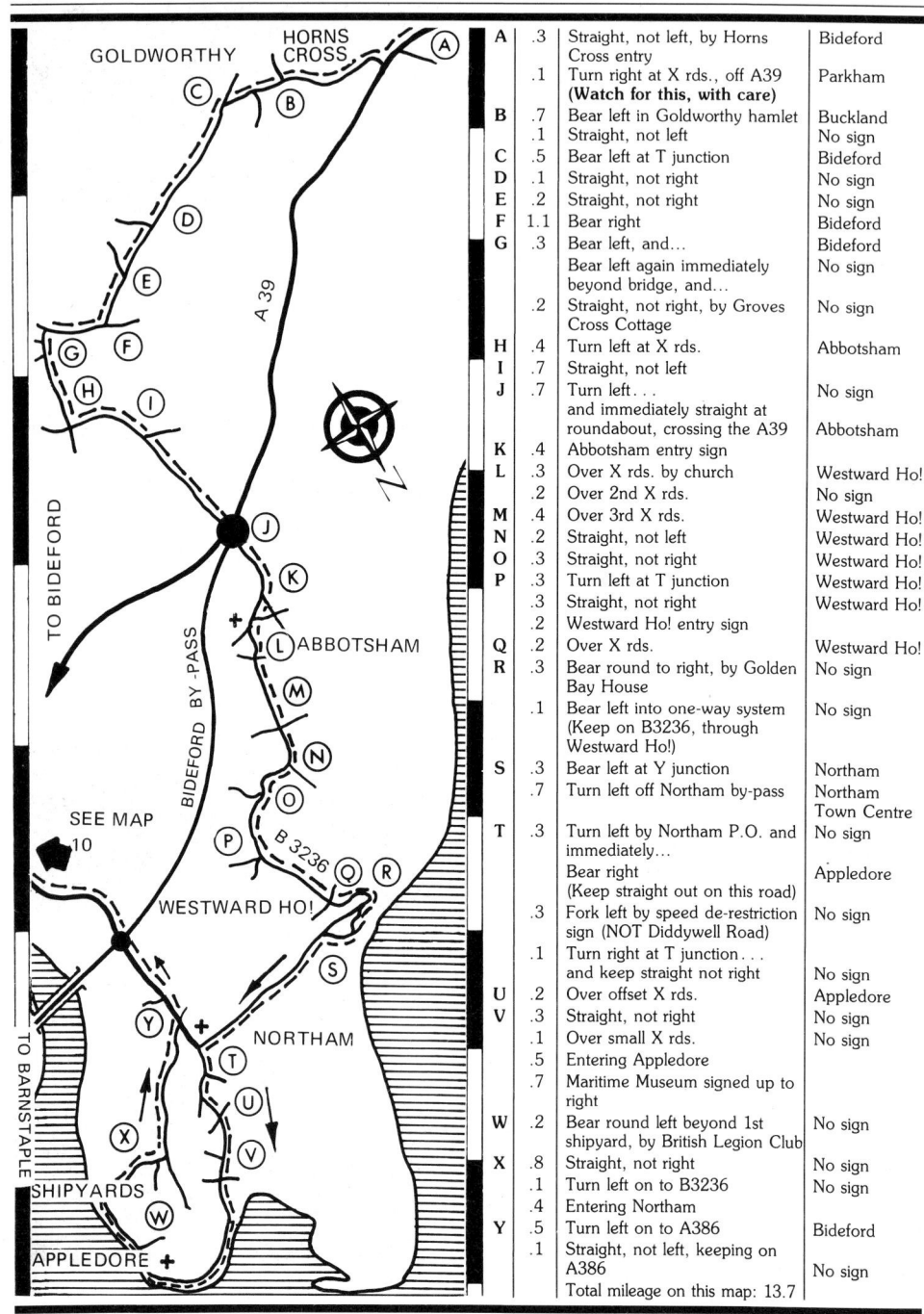

CROWN COPYRIGHT RESERVED

On Route

Horns Cross
Hamlet with an attractive hotel at its western end. This is the Hoops Inn, a long low thatched building, with a brightly painted coach in its colourful garden across the road.

Abbotsham
An unexciting village with considerable modern development, it has a stout well built church, which was much restored in 1870. However this still has a fine set of early 16th century bench ends, including a carving of a chained ape, believed to represent drunkeness. It is possible to walk to Abbotsham Cliffs, by following the path that starts close to Abbotsham Court Lodge. (Turn left at Point M.)

Westward Ho!
A development company established this 'settlement' in the 1860's and 70's, naming it after Charles Kingsley's book, which had been published in 1855. Kipling was educated at the United Services College (long since moved from here), and Kipling Torrs, to the west of the town, was the scene for many of the exploits of Stalky and Co. Standing on the grassy slopes of Kipling Torrs (now owned by The National Trust) we were delighted with the dramatic stretch of sands, extending northwards to the mouth of the Taw Torridge Estuary. These sands are backed by the long Pebble Ridge, nearly 2 miles in length and 20 feet high. (Turn left about ½ mile beyond Point S, to visit Northam Burrows and the Pebble Ridge.)

The architectural merits of Westward Ho! are strictly limited, but those in search of late Victorian period flavour will be adequately rewarded. Let us move to Northam without further comment.

Northam
Large village with views northwards over the green expanse of Northam Burrows (Golf, Bird Life, Ponies and an extensive Rubbish Dump), and much ugly development upon its fringes. However there is a lively busy atmosphere in its little square, which is overlooked by a tall towered church (used as a shipping mark for centuries). Its large interior was heavily restored in the mid-19th century, and contains only a few items of interest.

Appledore
Overlooks the broad tidal waters marking the union of Taw and Torridge before they pour out to sea through a narrow channel into Bideford Bay. There are splendid open views over the water to Braunton Burrows, and across the wide sands to Instow. Although it includes the West Country's most successful small shipyard, Appledore retains a pleasantly relaxed air, with a broad quay overlooked by steeply sited Georgian and early Victorian cottages. In summer the quay is busy with small boats and there is a ferry across to sandy Instow. Do not miss a visit to the Maritime Museum, in Odun Road.

1. The Hoops Inn, Horns Cross

2. Westward Ho! Beach

3. On Appledore Quay

4. Alleyway at Appledore   5. Alleyway at Appledore

Map 10

	kms Ref. Miles	Directions	Sign-posted
	.3	Keep straight into Bideford centre on A386 going over roundabout	Bideford
	.3	Entering Bideford	
A	1.0	Turn left at roundabout and cross bridge over Torridge, on A39	Barnstaple
B	.2	Turn left at mini-roundabout	Barnstaple
C	.2	Fork right, off, A39 *before de-restriction signs.* (WATCH FOR THIS, WITH CARE) (But go straight ahead on A39 if you wish to visit Tapeley Park... on right after 1.8 miles)	'Old Barnstaple Road'
D	1.3	Over small X rds.	No sign
E	.2	Straight, not left	No sign
F	.2	Straight, not right	No sign
G	.2	Straight, not left	Barnstaple
	.1	Eastleigh entry signed	
H	.6	Turn right at T junction	Horwood
	.6	Horwood entry signed	
I	.1	Straight, not right, beyond church	Lovacott
J	1.2	Turn left at X rds. in Lower Lovacott	Fremington
K	.4	Straight, not left, and almost immediately...	Barnstaple
		Bear right	No sign
L	.6	Turn sharp right, on to B3232	Newton Tracey
M	.2	Bear left, off B3232 (WATCH FOR THIS, WITH CARE)	No sign
N	.5	Over small X rds.	New Bridge
O	.3	Turn left at T junction (WATCH FOR THIS, WITH CARE)	Collabear
P	.4	Turn left at T junction by farm	Tawstock
Q	.6	Straight, not left	No sign
R	.3	Turn right at T junction	Tawstock
S	.2	Straight, not right, in Tawstock	Barnstaple
T	.1	Fork left by phone box (But bear right to visit Tawstock church, etc... about ¼ mile)	No sign
	.7	Tower in field on left	
	.6	Over roundabout	
U	.6	Turn right on to A39 at entry to Barnstaple	No sign
	.3	Over mini roundabout, over bridge, and...	Town Centre
		Total mileage on this map: 12.5	

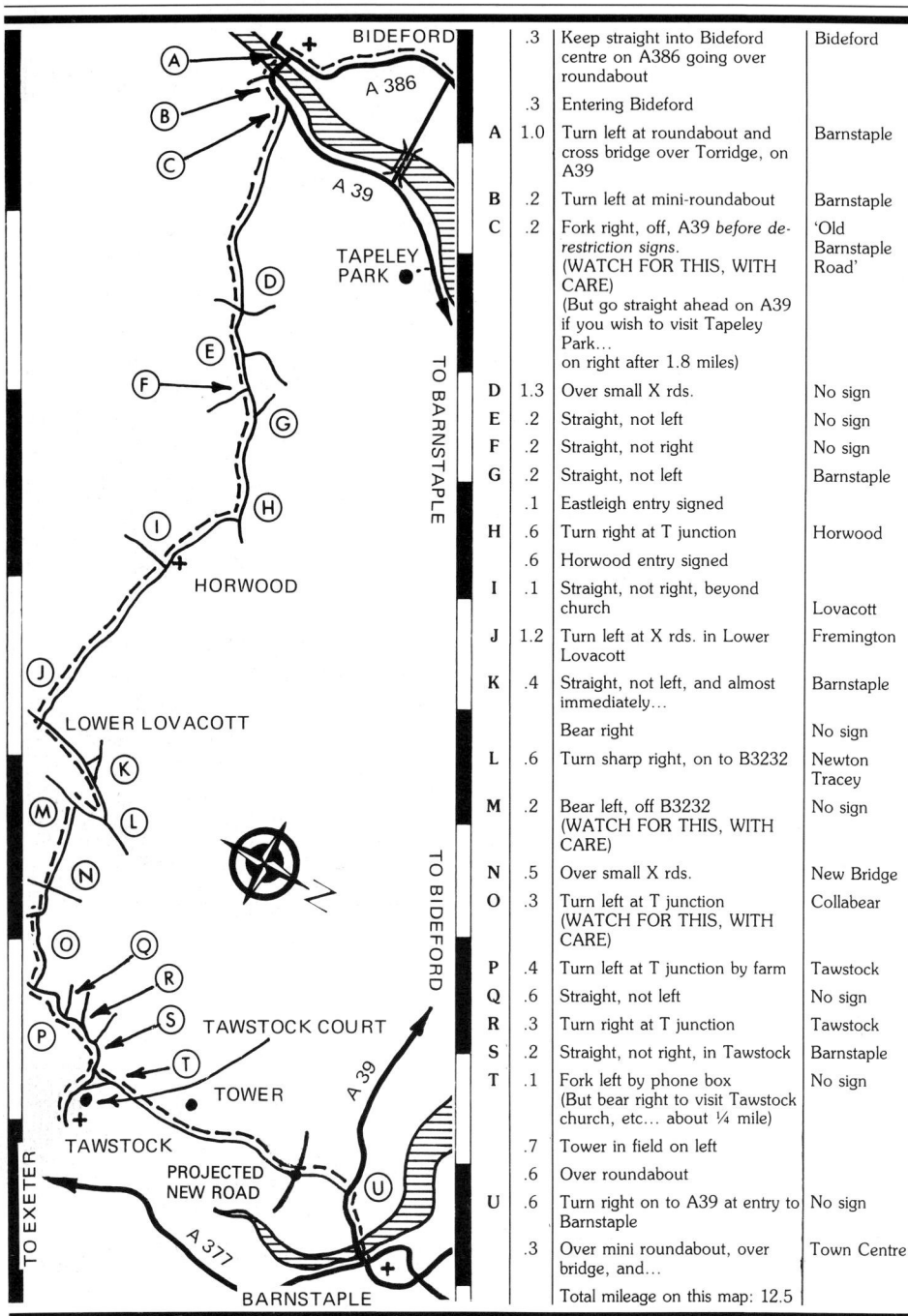

CROWN COPYRIGHT RESERVED

On Route

Bideford

Bright, attractive town built on a hillside sloping down to its long tree lined quay on the Torridge, crossed here by a stout 24 arch bridge. This dates back to the 14th century, but has a long history of widening and repairs (the most recent being in 1968, when it had to be closed for three months). A new bridge carrying a bypass is now open.

Bideford was a port of real significance from the days of the Grenvilles (Sir Richard's 'Revenge' was crewed by Bideford men) until its decline in the early 19th century, when trade shifted to Bristol, Liverpool and London. However Bideford Quay still handles coasting trade, and small timber ships from the Baltic may often be seen alongside.

Apart from its bridge and quay, Bideford has pleasant sloping streets with cheerful shops and elegant houses (see especially Bridgeland Street). The church is dull, but there is a small Art Gallery, backing onto Victoria Park, at the north end of the quay.

Tapeley Park

A largely Georgian mansion with a restored neo-Georgian facing, and containing fine plasterwork ceilings, furniture and porcelain. There is a long drive with rhododendrons, formal 'Italian Gardens' complete with statuary and palm trees. There are splendid views out across the Taw and Torridge estuary to Appledore and Braunton Burrows. The Queen Anne Dairy tea room is open for refreshments, and there is a plant and produce shop, and a picnic area.

Horwood

Has a small church, inside which there is a delightful effigy of a 15th century lady in alabaster, set beneath a window. This is situated in the north aisle, which was built by John Pollard and the effigy is thought to be that of his wife Emma. There are also some interesting bench ends and a Jacobean pulpit and altar rail. Do not overlook the attractive thatched cottage next to the church.

Tawstock

Quiet little thatched village with an 18th century Gothick mansion on a hill above. This is Tawstock Court, and was built in 1787 to replace an earlier house, of which only the splendid gatehouse (1574) survives. This is at the roadside on our diversion to the church, which is itself beautifully sited on the slopes of a small coombe overlooking the broad Taw valley.

Tawstock church dates largely from the 14th century and has an interior unspoilt by over-restoration. It contains a bewildering quantity of beautiful things, which include a series of splendid monuments to successive owners of Tawstock... The Fitzwarrens, the Bourchiers and the Wreys. Also do not miss the lovely plastered ceilings of the transepts, the little galleried walk to the tower, and the carved manorial pew. A visit here is highly recommended.

1. Bideford Quay

2. Cottage at Horwood

3. Tawstock Church

Map 11

Ref.	kms/Miles	Directions	Sign-posted
A	.1	Turn left beyond bridge (Or link in with Map 1, Point A, by going round the Square, and heading out on A361, following signs to Taunton)	Lynton
B	.4	Straight over traffic lights, and almost immediately...	Lynton
	.1	Turn left at T junction	Lynton
C	.1	Bear left, off A39, and immediately...	Pilton
		Bear right	Pilton
D	.2	Turn left just before Pilton church	No sign
	.1	Bear left	'Under Minnow Rd'
E	.2	Over offset X rds.	No sign
	.1	Windsor Arms on right	
	.5	Upcott House just visible ahead left	
F	.4	Fork left	Ashford
G	.4	Over X rds.	Braunton
H	1.1	Turn sharp left at X rds.	Ashford
I	.4	Turn right at X rds.	Heanton
	1.2	Heanton entry signed	
J	.1	Straight, not left	No sign
	.1	Church on right	
K	.1	Bear left by phone box	No sign
L	.5	Turn right at T junction by Heanton Church Rooms, and immediately...	No sign
		Straight, not left by the Williams Arms, in Braunton	No sign
	.3	Straight, not left	No sign
M	.3	Fork left, and bear left, down Heanton Street	Saunton
N	.1	Turn right at X rds. onto A361	No sign
		Then turn left at traffic lights on to B3231	Saunton
	.1	On left large car park and beyond this a turning on left for Broughton Marsh and Burrows. (But we recommend the alternative road from point P)	
		Keep straight out of Broughton on B3231	
O	.6	Straight, not left	No sign
P	.6	Over offset X rds. (But turn left to visit Braunton Burrows)	No sign
	.1	Saunton entry signed	
	1.0	Bridle Path to Saunton Sands on left	
		Total mileage on this map: 9.2	

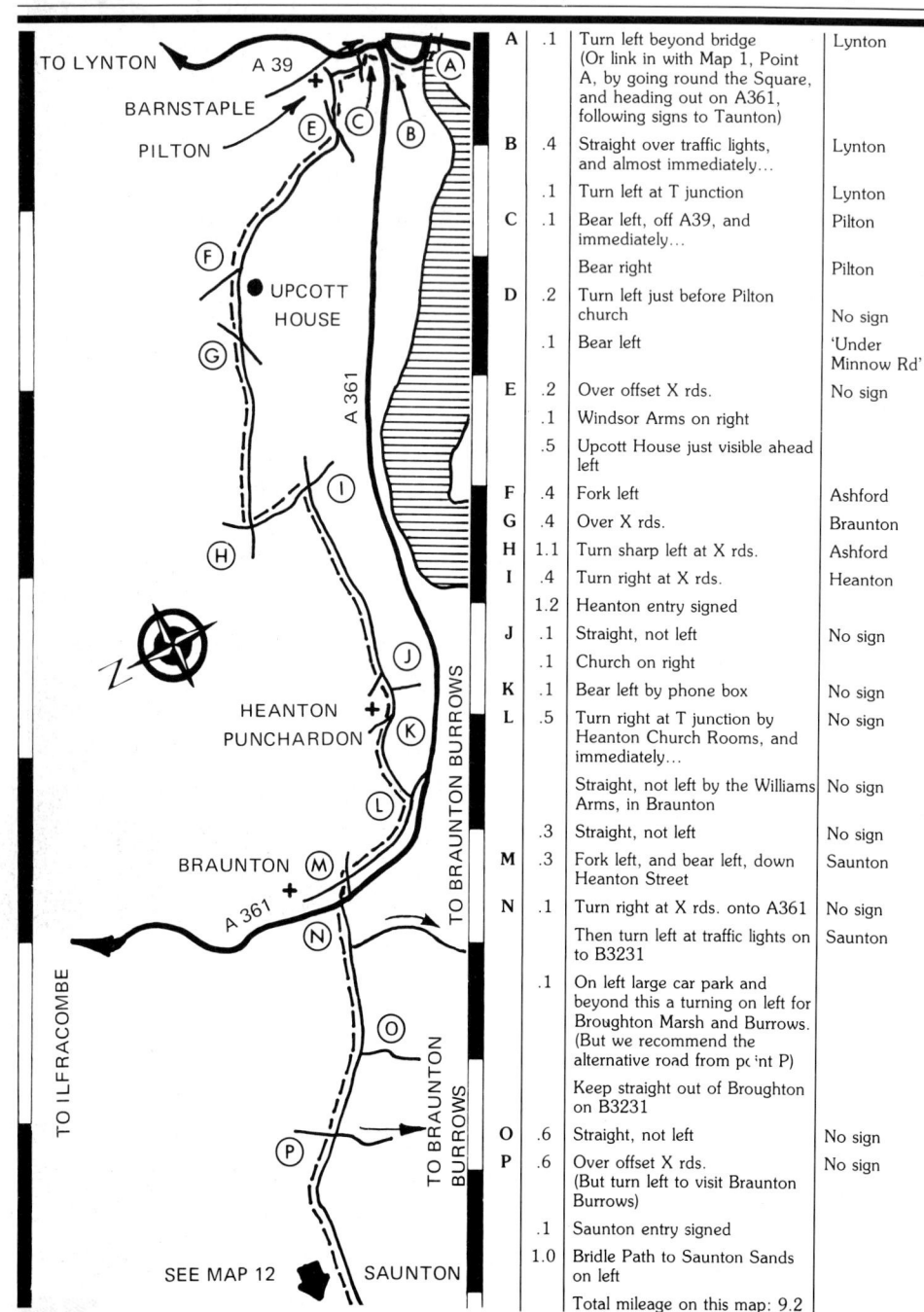

CROWN COPYRIGHT RESERVED

On Route

Pilton

Was more important than Barnstaple in Saxon times, and although it now appears on the map to be no more than a suburb of Barnstaple, it has retained a highly individual flavour. There are several pleasant old stone houses near the church, which is itself best approached beneath the archway in the convincingly 'antique' 19th century almshouses. From here one walks up a cobbled pathway to the south door.

The church was a priory church of the Benedictines until the Dissolution in 1536 and although much altered about that time, there are still signs of its 13th century origins. The Chichester family purchased Pilton Priory and evidence of their connection with Pilton is provided by the two splendid monuments, to Sir John Chichester (1569) and Sir Robert (1627). See also the ornate font cover, with a canopy similar to that at Swimbridge (See Page 3), the 16th century stone pulpit, the fine rood screen, and the monument to Christopher Lethbridge.

Heanton Punchardon

Small village sited at the end of a 200 foot high ridge overlooking the Taw estuary. There are splendid sweeping views towards the Clovelly cliffs and in the churchyard there are buried many young men from the Dominions who were stationed at nearby Chivenor airfield during the 1939–45 War. The Perpendicular church has a tall west tower and a beautiful white plastered interior, enriched by several interesting monuments. See especially the 16th century canopied tomb to Richard Coffin.

Braunton

Claims to the England's largest village (population about 4,000) and has grown to this size as a dormitory to Barnstaple. However the old part of the village at the northern end, in a valley overlooked by a ruined chapel, is reasonably attractive. The church, like Barnstaple and Swimbridge, has a lead covered medieval spire, and in addition, a stream flowing beside its churchyard. Inside it has a massive wagon roof and a fine collection of carved bench ends, although it lacks much warmth of feeling.

Braunton Burrows
(KEEP CLEAR IF RED FLAG IS FLYING)

(Turn left beyond Car Park in Braunton or turn left at Point P.)

A wonderful desert landscape with dunes stretching southwards for almost three miles, to Airy Point, at the confluence of the Taw and Torridge. The great stretch of Saunton Sands lies about a mile to the west of the road, and between the dunes rise to over 70 feet. To the east lies the flat green Braunton Marsh, with its little reed lined drainage canals. Opportunities for bird watching are excellent, especially in winter. Please respect Nature Reserve's requirements.

1. Churchyard Path, Barnstaple

2. South porch, Pilton

3. At Braunton Burrows

Map 12

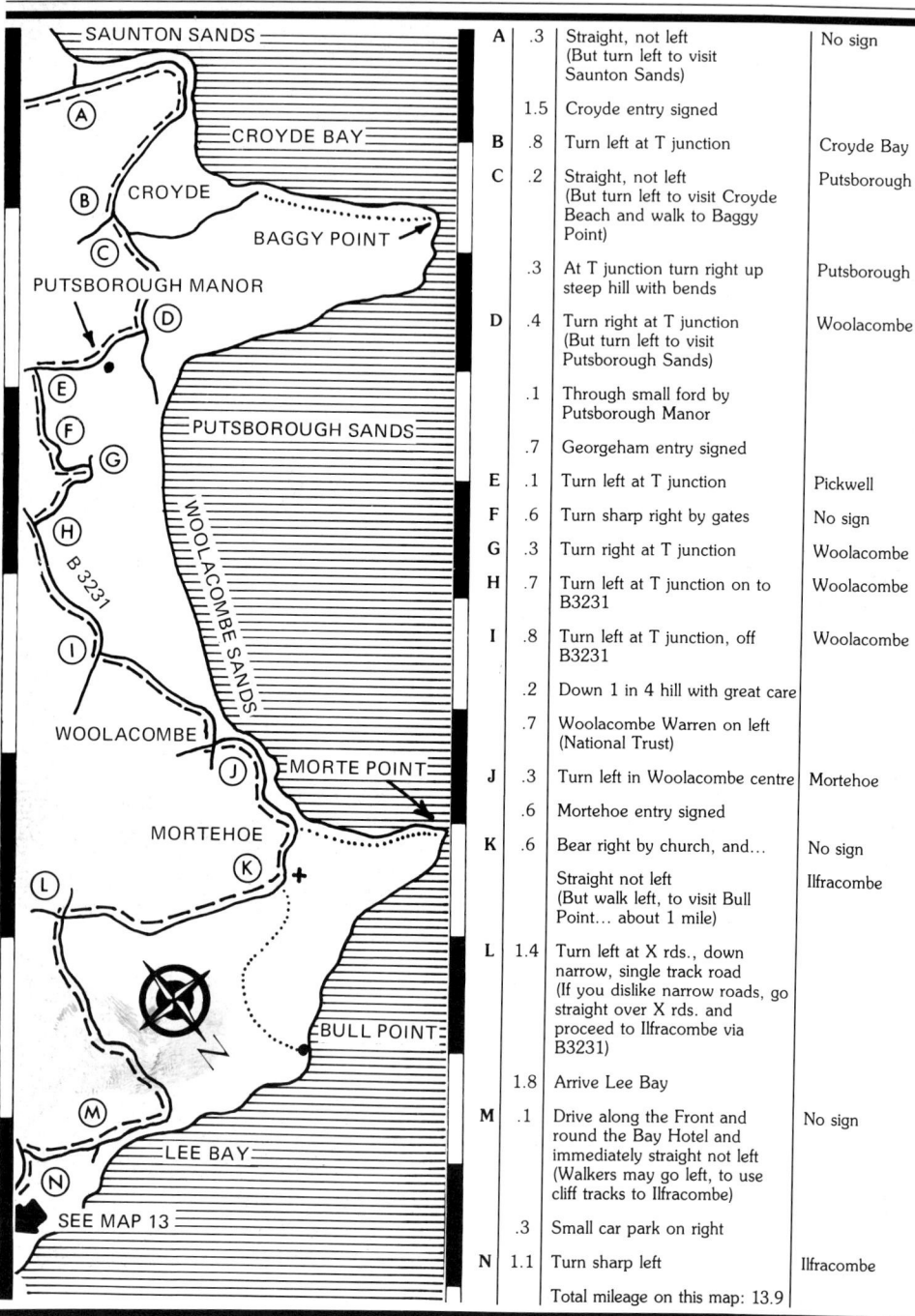

Ref.	kms / Miles	Directions	Signposted
A	.3	Straight, not left (But turn left to visit Saunton Sands)	No sign
	1.5	Croyde entry signed	
B	.8	Turn left at T junction	Croyde Bay
C	.2	Straight, not left (But turn left to visit Croyde Beach and walk to Baggy Point)	Putsborough
	.3	At T junction turn right up steep hill with bends	Putsborough
D	.4	Turn right at T junction (But turn left to visit Putsborough Sands)	Woolacombe
	.1	Through small ford by Putsborough Manor	
	.7	Georgeham entry signed	
E	.1	Turn left at T junction	Pickwell
F	.6	Turn sharp right by gates	No sign
G	.3	Turn right at T junction	Woolacombe
H	.7	Turn left at T junction on to B3231	Woolacombe
I	.8	Turn left at T junction, off B3231	Woolacombe
	.2	Down 1 in 4 hill with great care	
	.7	Woolacombe Warren on left (National Trust)	
J	.3	Turn left in Woolacombe centre	Mortehoe
	.6	Mortehoe entry signed	
K	.6	Bear right by church, and...	No sign
		Straight not left (But walk left, to visit Bull Point... about 1 mile)	Ilfracombe
L	1.4	Turn left at X rds., down narrow, single track road (If you dislike narrow roads, go straight over X rds. and proceed to Ilfracombe via B3231)	
	1.8	Arrive Lee Bay	
M	.1	Drive along the Front and round the Bay Hotel and immediately straight not left (Walkers may go left, to use cliff tracks to Ilfracombe)	No sign
	.3	Small car park on right	
N	1.1	Turn sharp left	Ilfracombe
		Total mileage on this map: 13.9	

CROWN COPYRIGHT RESERVED

On Route

Saunton Sands
These fabulous sands stretch nearly three miles southwards from our road, and are backed by the great dunes of Braunton (See Page 23). Walk the three miles south to the little lighthouse at Airy Point.

Croyde
A 'pretty' village with thatched cottages and a small clear stream. It is crowded at holiday times but away from the coast it has withstood the pressures of tourism, and shown praise-worthy restraint.

Croyde Bay
Small sandy bay, reasonably sheltered from the north wind, with considerable 'holiday development'. Surfing and sandcastle building good here.

Baggy Point
An attractive rocky headland owned by The National Trust, about a mile's walk beyond Croyde Bay. It is possible to continue one's walk to Putsborough Sands and beyond to Woolacombe.

Putsborough
Picturesque hamlet with a thatched manor house overlooking a small ford. Nearby Putsborough Sands lie at south end of Woolacombe Sands (See below).

Woolacombe
A holiday village, which despite later developments, has retained a strong Edwardian flavour. It lies in a wide combe at the northern end of the splendid two mile long Woolacombe Sands, and is backed by high downs. Swimming, surfing and superb castle building ensure its popularity, and those who dislike crowds have ample space in which to manoeuvre.

Shell Beach
Lying in Combesgate between Woolacombe and Mortehoe, this small sheltered beach is noted for the wonderful variety of its shells.

Morte Point
There are find views of this treacherous, rocky headland from Shell Beach, but it is best reached by a path starting near Mortehoe church.

Mortehoe
Pleasant coastal village with a small scale church of Norman origin, situated in a minute churchyard. See especially the fine altar tomb of William de Tracey (1322), the carved bench ends, and the impressive mosaic over the chancel arch.

Bull Point Lighthouse
This must be reached on foot either from Morte Point (see above), or from Mortehoe (Point K).

Lee Bay
Minute rocky bay backed by a long wooded valley. There is fine walking westwards to Bull Point via Damage Cliffs, or eastwards to Ilfracombe via Torrs Walk. At Lee Bay there are tea gardens, the well known 'Old Maid's Cottage', a 'smuggler's cottage' and at nearby Sandy Cove, a small beach.

1. Saunton Sands

2. Croyde Bay

3. The Road to Putsborough Sands

4. Lee Bay

Map 13

kms Ref. Miles	Directions	Sign-posted
	1.0	Entering Ilfracombe	
A	.6	Turn sharp right at X rds.	Richmond Road
	.1	Turn left at T junction	No sign
	.2	Go straight ahead, WITH GREAT CARE, joining A361 and A399 (Keep on A399 right through Ilfracombe, following signs marked Combe Martin) (But turn left if you wish to visit beaches or harbour)	Combe Martin
B	.8	Fork left	Combe Martin
C	.2	Straight, not right (But turn right to visit Chambercombe Manor... .4)	No sign
	.5	Hele Mill down to right	
	1.2	Watermouth Bay now visible to left	
	.5	Watermouth Castle up on right	
	.1	Entrance to Watermouth Cove on left	
D	.4	Fork right, off A399	Berrynarbour
E	.5	Straight, not right at entry to Berrynarbour	Berrrynarbour
F	.2	Turn left after passing church	Combe Martin
G	.6	Turn right, re-joining A399	Combe Martin
	.3	Entry to Combe Martin signed	
		Keep straight into village	
H	.9	Turn left into Shute Lane just beyond Rone House Hotel which is on right (WATCH FOR THIS WITH GREAT CARE)	No sign
	.6	Splendid view back towards bay	
	.3	Ruined mine buildings over to right	
	.3	Path on left to the Great Hangman, and...	
I		Straight, not right	No sign
J	1.2	Turn left at X rds.	Trentishoe
	.7	Footpath to Holdstone Hill on left	
		Fine views southwards to Exmoor	
		Total mileage on this map: 11.4	

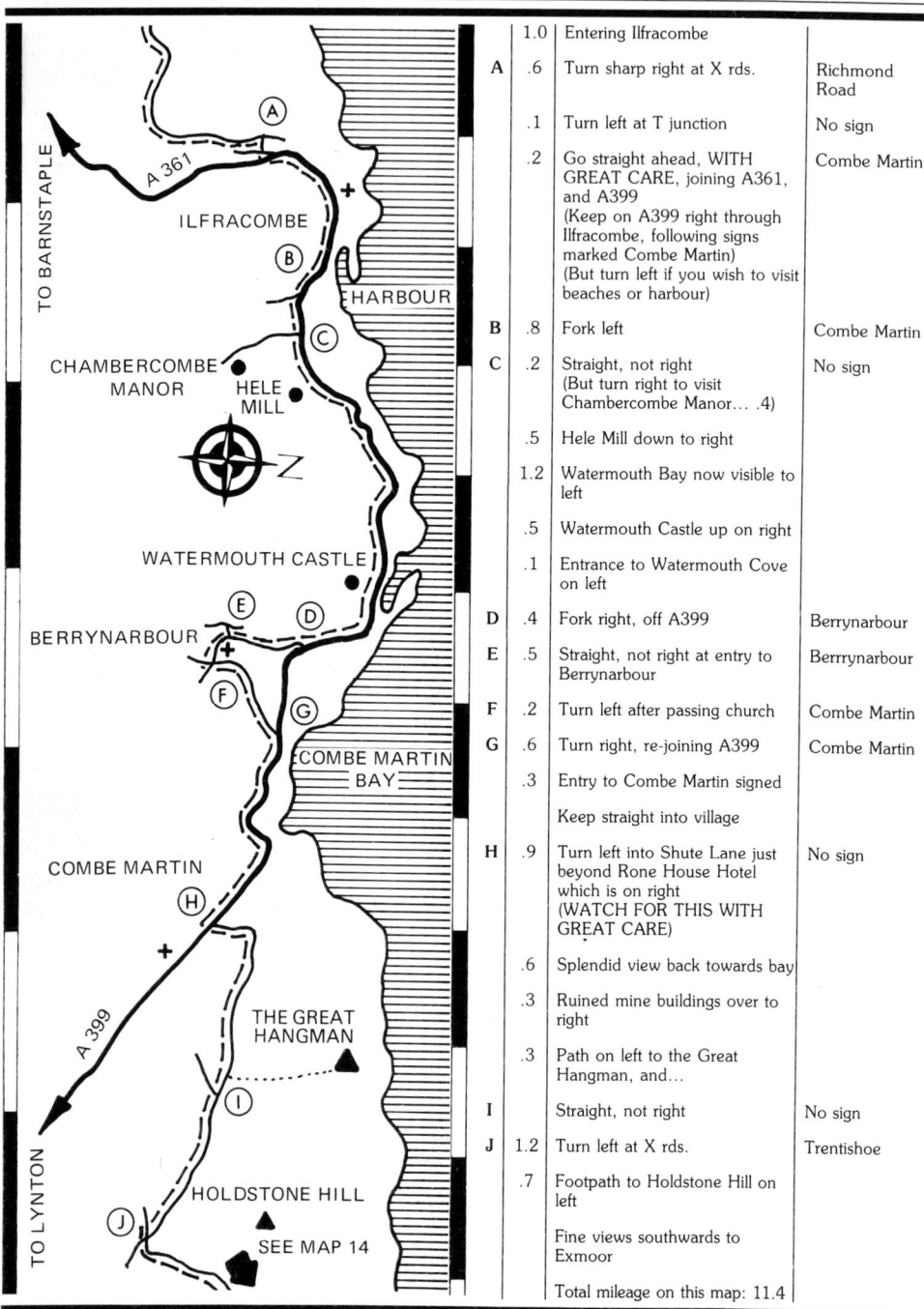

CROWN COPYRIGHT RESERVED

On Route

Ilfracombe

Its harbour was developed by the Bourchiers (Earls of Bath) of Tawstock, but it never achieved the importance of Bideford or Barnstaple as a seaport. However its splendidly romantic setting soon attracted the attention of the early 'holiday makers' and it developed rapidly throughout the last half of the nineteenth century. This is all too evident in the almost exclusively Victorian character of the town, but the bright little harbour, the small beach and dramatic cliff walks make Ilfracombe well worth visiting (avoid peak holiday times if possible).

Climb up to St. Nicholas Chapel, a lighthouse since the 18th century, to Hillsborough Hill, to Capstone Hill and to Torrs Walk to the west of the town, from whence one can walk to Lee Bay (See Page 25). There is a small museum and Ilfracombe is also the best departure point for Lundy Island, for South Wales, or for a cruise along the North Devon coast.

Chambercombe Manor

A delightful manor farm house, situated in a quiet valley behind Ilfracombe. The house is set amongst lovely informal gardens, with a tea garden in a courtyard, complete with a fountain and weeping willow.

Hele Mill

Charming little restored watermill dating back to 1525. There is an 18 ft. overshot water wheel, and many interesting items inside. Wholemeal flour is produced and is of course on sale.

Watermouth

Gothick Watermouth Castle was built in 1825 and overlooks beautiful Watermouth Bay. The Castle has been transformed into a large and attractive family entertainment complex, with a host of features. Do not miss a visit here if you are looking for light-hearted fun.

Berrynarbour

The lofty red sandstone tower of the church dominates the centre of this delightful small village. If visiting the church do not miss the attractive monument to Richard Berry (1645), and the arcading of Beer stone.

Combe Martin

A long thin village straggling down a narrow valley, which ends at a small bay with some sand at low tide. Combe Martin is renowned for its splendid coastal scenery, and it is possible to walk up north-eastwards to the Little Hangman Hill, and on to the Great Hangman. Holdstone Hill is best reached by walking to the left of our route after passing POINT J. There are splendid views of the Welsh coast from all three points.

Do not miss the Pack of Cards Inn, a folly built in the shape of a 'card house', nor the church with its fine 99-foot high tower, and its painted rood screen.

Combe Martin grew up as a mining town, and in medieval times was well known as a lead and silver producing centre. Mining only ceased here in the 1870's and there are still some remains to be seen (1 mile beyond POINT H.)

1. Coastline at Ilfracombe

2. Ilfracombe Harbour

3. Hele Mill

4. Combe Martin Coastline

Map 14

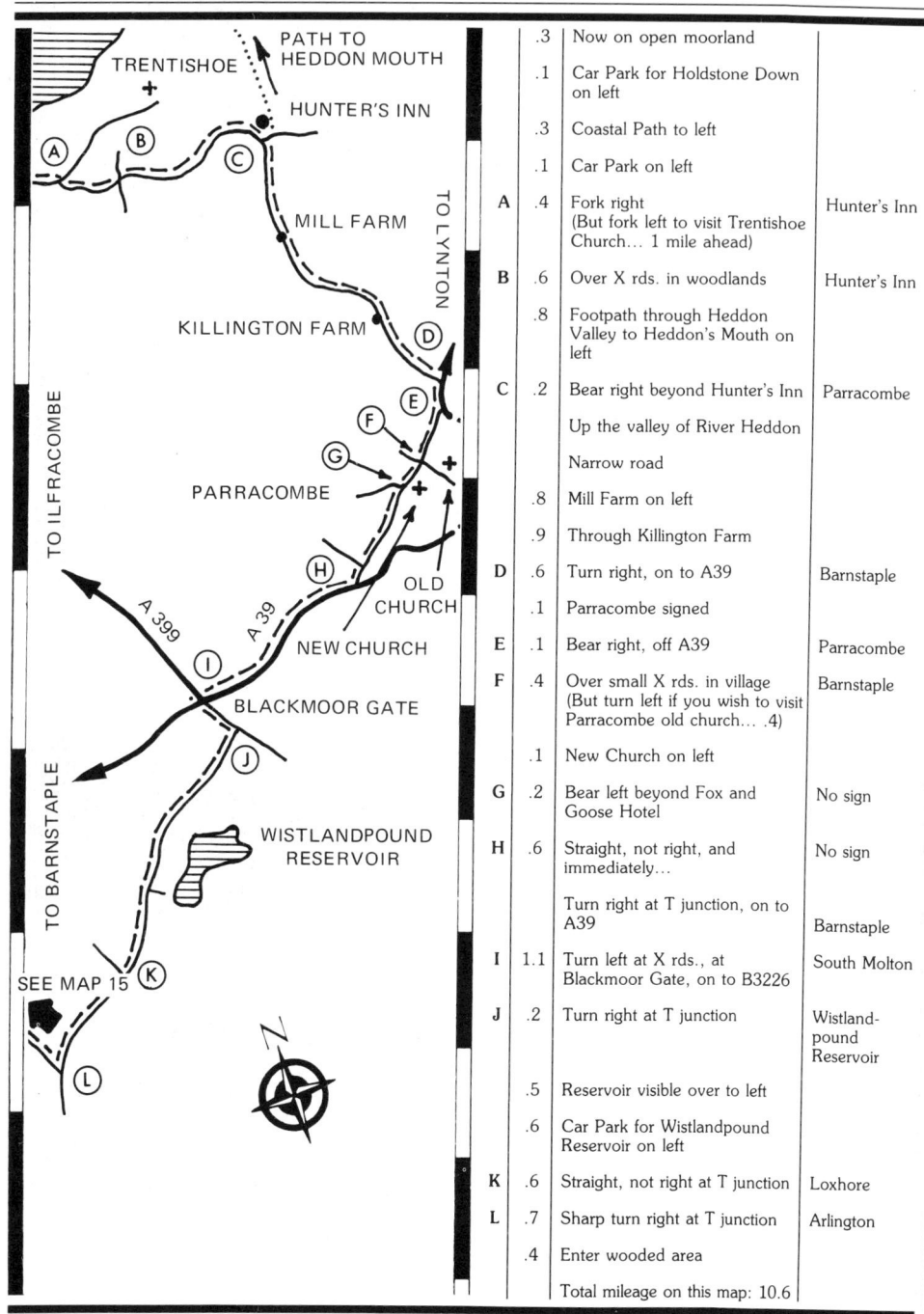

Miles / kms Ref. Miles / Directions / Signposted

		Directions	Signposted
	.3	Now on open moorland	
	.1	Car Park for Holdstone Down on left	
	.3	Coastal Path to left	
	.1	Car Park on left	
A	.4	Fork right (But fork left to visit Trentishoe Church... 1 mile ahead)	Hunter's Inn
B	.6	Over X rds. in woodlands	Hunter's Inn
	.8	Footpath through Heddon Valley to Heddon's Mouth on left	
C	.2	Bear right beyond Hunter's Inn	Parracombe
		Up the valley of River Heddon	
		Narrow road	
	.8	Mill Farm on left	
	.9	Through Killington Farm	
D	.6	Turn right, on to A39	Barnstaple
	.1	Parracombe signed	
E	.1	Bear right, off A39	Parracombe
F	.4	Over small X rds. in village (But turn left if you wish to visit Parracombe old church... .4)	Barnstaple
	.1	New Church on left	
G	.2	Bear left beyond Fox and Goose Hotel	No sign
H	.6	Straight, not right, and immediately...	No sign
		Turn right at T junction, on to A39	Barnstaple
I	1.1	Turn left at X rds., at Blackmoor Gate, on to B3226	South Molton
J	.2	Turn right at T junction	Wistlandpound Reservoir
	.5	Reservoir visible over to left	
	.6	Car Park for Wistlandpound Reservoir on left	
K	.6	Straight, not right at T junction	Loxhore
L	.7	Sharp turn right at T junction	Arlington
	.4	Enter wooded area	
		Total mileage on this map: 10.6	

Map labels: TRENTISHOE; PATH TO HEDDON MOUTH; HUNTER'S INN; MILL FARM; TO LYNTON; KILLINGTON FARM; PARRACOMBE; OLD CHURCH; NEW CHURCH; A399; A39; BLACKMOOR GATE; WISTLANDPOUND RESERVOIR; TO ILFRACOMBE; TO BARNSTAPLE; SEE MAP 15

CROWN COPYRIGHT RESERVED

On Route

Trentishoe Church

A small building sheltering close to a farm, at the head of a valley running northwards and therefore seemingly remote from the sea. It has been over restored inside with glossy tiles and pitch-pine pews, but it has a delightful little musician's gallery, so small that a hole had to be cut into the parapet to accommodate the double-bass!

Hunter's Inn

Is situated in the thickly wooded valley of the River Heddon, about a mile to the south of Heddon's Mouth. The walk down the sheltered valley (either side of the river) to the wild shoreline at the Mouth provides a wonderful contrast in scenery, but to enjoy the full opportunities offered to walkers, purchase the excellent Map Guide to Woody Bay and Heddon's Mouth, published by The National Trust. If exploring the shoreline from Heddon's Mouth, make quite certain that you are not involved with a rising tide.

Parracombe

Small village tucked away in the valley of the Heddon, only two miles from its source, 1,300 feet up on Exmoor. The main road and the course of the old Lynton–Barnstaple Railway (see below) curve around the hillside above it, and between the two is situated Parracombe's old church. This was almost demolished in 1878, when the New Church was built, but a 'protest' by John Ruskin, among others, led to its rescue.

Having never been 'restored' by unsympathetic Victorians, it remains as one of the few churches with an unspoilt 17th and 18th century interior, with box pews, a screen with tympanum, and a pulpit with reader's and clerk's pews attached. This little church is full of character and is well worth the short diversion from our route. If you find it locked enquire at one of the nearby cottages.

Lynton and Barnstaple Railway

Signs of this railway may still be spotted to the right of the A39 before reaching Blackmoor Gate, although it closed in 1936. This two foot gauge miniature railway was opened in 1898, and although it never paid its way, it must have provided visitors with a delightful scenic run. Close by Parracombe Church the Lynton and Barnstaple Garden Railway utilises a quarter of a mile of the former track to show models of the old railway stock in a 'Garden Railway,' and along the old track bed there are wild flowers growing among features of the old railway which have been left in situ.

Wistlandpound Reservoir

An attractive 'lake' in the hills, with tree clad banks, and fine views over rolling country westwards. Fishing permits are available near the lakeside.

1. Trentishoe Church

2. Hunter's Inn

3. Parracombe Old Church

4. Late Autumn at Wistlandpound

Map 15

Ref	kms/Miles	Directions	Signposted
A	.5	Turn right at T junction (But turn left to visit Arlington church)	No sign
	.3	Entry to Arlington Court on left...	
		Car Park on right	
B	.4	Turn left, on to A39	Barnstaple
C	.5	Turn left at T junction, keeping on A39	Barnstaple
	1.7	Old entrance Gates to Arlington Court on left. (NO ENTRY)	
D	.8	Straight, not right, keeping on A39	Barnstaple
E	.3	Turn left at X rds., off A39	No sign
F	.6	Turn left beyond Shirwell church	Loxhore
G	.5	Bear right at T junction	Loxhore
		Over bridge, and...	
H	.6	Turn right at T junction	Barnstaple
I	.1	Straight, not left	Bratton Fleming
J	.6	Bear right at T junction	Barnstaple
K	.6	Straight at T junction	Barnstaple
L	.1	Straight, not left, at Y junction, keeping on main road (We shall keep on this main road into Barnstaple)	No sign
M	.9	Straight, not right	No sign
N	1.3	Straight, not left	Barnstaple
O	.4	Straight, not left twice, where Barnstaple entry is signed	No sign
P	.5	Straight, not left	No sign
		Keep straight into Barnstaple	
Q	1.0	Turn left into one-way system	No sign
R	.2	Keep straight, not left, and follow into 'The Square', Barnstaple,	Ilfracombe
		BUT GO LEFT TO LINK WITH MAP 1 AND FOLLOW SIGNS FOR A361 TAUNTON	
		Total mileage on this map: 12.0	

TO LYNTON

ARLINGTON COURT

SHIRWELL

SNAPPER

BARNSTAPLE

TO ILFRACOMBE

TO BIDEFORD — A 39

A 377 TO EXETER

A 361 TO BAMPTON

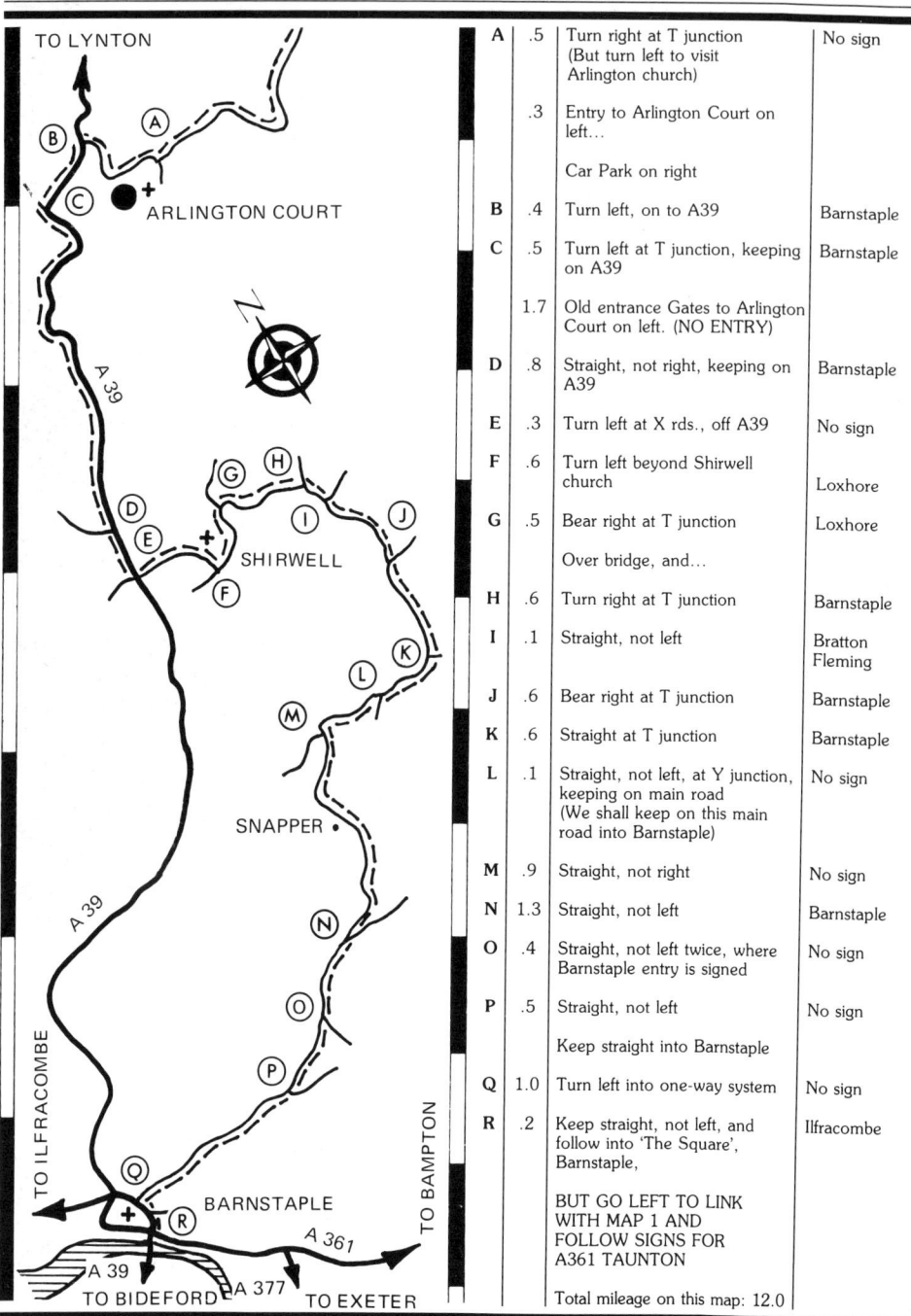

CROWN COPYRIGHT RESERVED

On Route

Arlington

The church and a few houses lie at the edge of Arlington Court's beautiful park. We came here first in February when bright sunshine lit up the small churchyard, with snowdrops carpeting the grass beyond a great yew tree's shadow. Apart from its tower the church was re-built in 1846, but it contains several monuments to the Chichesters. See especially the elegant monument to Mary Anne Chichester, and the monument by John Piper to Miss Rosalie, the last of the Chichesters of Arlington, to whom we are in debt for her most generous gift to the nation (See below).

1. Arlington Court

Arlington Court

The manor of Arlington was acquired by marriage in the 14th century, by the Chichester family, and they 'ruled' here from that time until 1947, when Miss Rosalie Chichester gave the estate to the National Trust, only two years before her death. Arlington Court was built in 1820–23 by Thomas Lee, a Barnstaple architect, and although it is of no great architectural merit, it is pleasantly sited on the edge of the park Miss Chichester maintained and developed so effectively between 1908 and 1947.

The interior of the house has a light, Edwardian flavour, and contains a fascinating collection of model ships (most extensive), shells, snuff boxes, pewter and porcelain, most of which had been amassed by Miss Rosalie. Do not miss the gorgeous red amber elephant, nor the silver model of Gipsy Moth IV, the boat which nephew, Sir Francis circum-navigated the world single handed.

There is a splendid collection of 19th century vehicles in the stables to the east of the church, a Nature Trail, taking about an hour, around the park, a restaurant and a shop selling guides and souvenirs. A herd of Shetland ponies and a flock of Jacob sheep graze in the park, through which it is possible to take a carriage ride.

Please allow yourselves plenty of time to visit this most interesting and well organised property, where nothing appears to be too much trouble for the quite exceptional staff.

2. Shirwell Porch

3. In Shirwell Churchyard

Shirwell

Small village lying to the west of the beautifully wooded valley of the Yeo. The church dates back to the 13th century, and its most unusual feature is a rough hewn timber pier supporting part of the north transept entrance. There is a 15th century effigy of a lady in the chancel, above which is a wall monument to Lady Anne Chichester (1723). Although this church was considerably restored in the 19th century it has retained a most pleasing atmosphere.

It was at Shirwell that Sir Francis Chichester spent much of his early years, as his father was rector here. Father and son are both buried in the churchyard.

4. Barnstaple Bridge

31

INDEX

	Page		Page
Abbotsham	19	Ebberly Arms	4
Abbotsham Cliffs	19	Ebberly House	7
Abbotsham Court	19	Elmscott	14
Acland, Sir Arthur	3	Exmanworthy Cliff	15
Airy Point	23, 25	Exmoor	29
Appledore	19	Fitzwarren Family	21
Arlington	31	Forda Farm	10
Arlington Court	31	Frithelstock	9
Ash	8	Frithelstock Priory	9
Atherington	5	Frithelstock Stone	6
Avery, Susannah	9	Gallantry Bower	15, 17
Bableigh Cross	2	Giffard Monument	5
Baggy Point	25	Gipsy Moth IV	31
Barnstaple	3, 23, 30	Goldworthy	18
Barnstaple Tiles	9, 11	Great Hangman Hill	27
Bath, Earl of	27	Grenville, Sir Bevil	11
Berry, Richard	27	Grenville, Sir Richard	21
Berrynarbour	27	Hamlyn Family	17
Bideford	21	Hamlyn, Sir James	17
Bideford Bay	17, 19	Hannaford	2
Bird Sanctuary	11	Hartland Abbey	9, 15
Black Horse Inn	7	Hartland Church	15
Blackmoor Gate	29	Hartland Forest Information Centre	15
Bourchier Family	21, 27	Hartland Point	15
Bradworthy	11	Hartland Quay	15
Braunton	23	Hartland Town	15
Braunton Burrows	19, 23	Hawker's Hut	13
Braunton Marsh	23	Hawker, The Rev. R.S.	13
Bridgeland Street	21	Heanton Punchardon	23
Brightly Barton	5	Heddon, River	29
Brownsham Farm	16	Heddon's Mouth	29
Bucks Mill	17	Hele Mill	27
Bude	13	Hembury Castle	9
Bull Point Lighthouse	25	Hilsborough Hill	27
Butcher's Row	3	High Bickington	7
Caledonia, The	13	Hobby Drive	17
Capstone Hill	27	Holdstone Hill	27
Cary Family	17	Hoops Inn	19
Chambercombe Manor	27	Horns Cross	19
Chapman Rock	15	Horwood	21
Charles II	11	Horwood's Almshouses	3
Chichester Family	23, 31	Hunters Inn	29
Chichester, Lady Anne	31	Ilfracombe	27
Chichester, Sir Francis	31	Instow	19
Chichester, Sir John	23	Jack Russell Inn	3
Chichester, Mary Anne	31	Kilkhampton	11
Chichester, Sir Robert	23	Killington Farm	28
Chichester, Miss Rosalie	31	Kingsley, Charles	17, 19
Chittlehampton	5	Kipling, Rudyard	19
Chivenor	23	Kipling Torrs	19
Churston Manor	9	Landkey	3
Clovelly	15, 17	Lee Bay	25
Clovelly Church	17	Lee, Thomas	31
Clovelly Cliffs	23	Lethbridge, Christopher	23
Clovelly Dykes	17	Little Hangman Hill	27
Coffin, Richard	23	Lovacott, Lower	20
Colscott	8	Lundy Island	15, 27
Combe Martin	27	Lymebridge	15
Combesgate	25	Lynton—Barnstaple Railway	29
Coombe	13	Marsland Mouth	13
Coombe Valley	13	Mortehoe	25
Croyde	25	Morte Point	25
Croyde Bay	25	Morwenstow	13
Damage Cliffs	25	Morwenstow Signal Station	13
Darracot	12	Mouth Mill	15, 17
Dartington Glass Works	7	Nature Reserve	23
Dartmoor	9	Nectan, St.	15
Davie, Charles	11	Nicholls, Anne and Susannah	11
De Tracey, William	25	Northam	19
Drymoors Cross	8	Northam Burrow	19
Duckpool Beach	13	Old Maid's Cottage	25
East Titchberry Farm	15	Pack of Cards Inn	27
Eastacott Cross	5	Palmer House	7
Eastcott	12	Parracombe	29